CAN'T BUY ME
LIKE

Bob Garfield and Doug Levy

CAN'T BUY ME
LIKE

HOW AUTHENTIC
CUSTOMER CONNECTIONS
DRIVE SUPERIOR RESULTS

PORTFOLIO / PENGUIN

PORTFOLIO / PENGUIN
Published by the Penguin Group
Penguin Group (USA) Inc., 375 Hudson Street, New York, New York 10014, U.S.A.
Penguin Group (Canada), 90 Eglinton Avenue East, Suite 700,
Toronto, Ontario, Canada M4P 2Y3 (a division of Pearson Penguin Canada Inc.)
Penguin Books Ltd, 80 Strand, London WC2R 0RL, England
Penguin Ireland, 25 St. Stephen's Green, Dublin 2, Ireland
(a division of Penguin Books Ltd)
Penguin Group (Australia), 707 Collins Street, Melbourne, Victoria 3008, Australia
(a division of Pearson Australia Group Pty Ltd)
Penguin Books India Pvt Ltd, 11 Community Centre, Panchsheel Park,
New Delhi – 110 017, India
Penguin Group (NZ), 67 Apollo Drive, Rosedale, Auckland 0632,
New Zealand (a division of Pearson New Zealand Ltd)
Penguin Books (South Africa), Rosebank Office Park, 181 Jan Smuts Avenue,
Parktown North 2193, South Africa
Penguin China, B7 Jiaming Center, 27 East Third Ring Road North, Chaoyang
District, Beijing 100020, China

Penguin Books Ltd, Registered Offices:
80 Strand, London WC2R 0RL, England

First published in 2013 by Portfolio / Penguin,
a member of Penguin Group (USA) Inc.

10 9 8 7 6 5 4 3 2 1

Copyright © Bob Garfield and Doug Levy, 2013
All rights reserved

"United Breaks Guitars" by Dave Carroll. Reprinted by permission of Dave Carroll.

Charts by MEplusYou

Photograph credits
Page 129: Erik Isakson/Getty Images
130 (top): Jupiterimages/Getty Images
130 (bottom): RunPhoto/Getty Images

LIBRARY OF CONGRESS CATALOGING IN PUBLICATION DATA

ISBN 978-1-591-84577-5

Printed in the United States of America
Set in Adobe Caslon Pro
Designed by Elyse Strongin, Neuwirth & Associates, Inc.

To our wives, Alyce and Milena

CONTENTS

CAN'T BUY ME
L✧KE

THE BOOK
YOU ARE READING

*My humanity is bound up in yours, for we can
only be human together.*

—DESMOND TUTU

The book you are reading is full of data, proprietary and public. It's rich with case histories of businesses, large and small. It comes complete with step-by-step instructions, like an IKEA bookcase or recipe for spaghetti Bolognese. We like to think it's also rather inspiring. But, at the most basic level, *Can't Buy Me Like* is a book about a simple truth: If you are still selling goods and services by blanketing the world with advertising, trying to persuade or entertain or flatter consumers into submission, you are doing things all wrong. Because the world has changed. A lot.

The old ways belong to a faraway time, kind of like Betamax and Yugoslavia. Whole industries continue to cling to the remnants of the status quo, but their grip gets ever weaker. The digital revolution and societal shifts have brought us to a new period. It is called the Relationship Era.

Don't worry. Confounding as change has been for business, this is a good-news tale. Technology hasn't sent us all plunging into *The*

1

Matrix or some other nightmarish techno-dystopia. On the contrary, in a happy paradox, we're being transported back to a more humane future. The digital revolution that has been so disruptive to business as usual has not merely multiplied the channels of communication between a consumer and consumer brands; it has launched us all into an era in which human needs, human values and human connections will define success or failure for those brands. The currency of Relationship Era marketing is not awareness, nor even quality; it is authenticity. Trust. Loyalty. Pride. Yes, you've gotta have the goods, but public expectations have changed and those qualities are now *part of* the goods. Commerce can no longer be about manipulating people into purchases. Relationship Era marketers do not see purchasers as conquests to seduce, or even persuade. They see them as friends—members of a community dedicated not only to the same stuff but to the same ideals. And this community is not confined to customers and prospects any more than the world itself is confined to customers and prospects. In the Relationship Era, your essence is transmitted in your relations with all stakeholders: customers, employees, suppliers, shareholders, neighbors and the earth itself. In short: Across every function of an enterprise, corporations and their brands now can and must behave with their various constituencies in ways *exactly parallel to human relationships.*

Across every function of an enterprise, corporations and their brands now can and must behave with their various constituencies in ways *exactly parallel to human relationships.*

And no amount of image advertising can paper over the gap between rhetoric and reality. Look around you. Signs of the paradigm shift are everywhere.

Just for Instance

You are no doubt familiar with Flo, the irrepressibly cheerful spokes-character for Progressive Insurance. She's the saleswoman in the heavenly Progressive "store," squeaky with delight at being able to help customers with their insurance needs. It's easy to love Flo, not only for her over-the-top exuberance but for her adorable devotion to her employer—the incandescence of which adoration, *plus $1 billion in media spending on her since 2008*, invited the public, too, to see Progressive in a flattering white light. All of which was fine, until the public was presented a reason to think differently. That took place in August 2012, when blogger Matt Fisher called out the insurance company for its conduct in the vehicular death of his sister and Progressive policyholder Kaitlynn Fisher. To keep from paying policy benefits, Matt alleged in a blog post, Progressive cheerfully appeared in court on behalf of the man who'd run a red light and killed their own customer.

Social media went predictably ballistic. And who took the brunt of the abuse? Flo, the fictional face of the company, created to distract us from what goes on in the back office behind the shiny store.

13 Aug@Stepto In other news @progressive's behavior has finally cured me of my attraction to Flo.

13 Aug@NickadooLA I wasn't surprised to hear Progressive's Flo killed all those people.

14 Aug@iamledgin The worst Progressive commercial is the one where Flo kills that guy's sister.

14 Aug@EricDSnider I happen to know that Flo chick is also Progressive's CEO, so if you see her, punch her in the face.

And with that, two things happened: Progressive was obliged to pay the Fisher family, and Flo virtually disappeared from view—a billion-dollar investment forced, at least temporarily, into hiding, like a fugitive or a snitch. That backlash was the direct and inevitable result of fabricating a brand image that did not square with reality. In today's world, reality will always catch up, and when it does—if the public feels hoodwinked—the damage will be irreparable. In the Relationship Era, brands can no longer project the image of their choosing. Rather, they must locate their inner selves and make common cause with the outside world. Yes, an entirely new way of doing business; what a nuisance.

In the Relationship Era, brands can no longer project the image of their choosing.

The Four Forces

This is no time, however, to be fretting about change. For one thing, like detours at construction sites, this shift is a temporary inconvenience for a permanent improvement. Whether you are the steward of a single brand, or a small business or a multinational corporation, embracing Relationship Era practices is sustainable in a way that even the most (superficially) efficient mass marketing never was. It also infuses business with meaning and values in a way the old model could never do. It also, as we shall demonstrate, enables you to maintain sales and growth trajectory at less expense. We will repeat that: *less expense*. Your authors are not quants, but we know this: All else being at least equal, reducing advertising costs increases return on investment correspondingly. The savings can then be plowed into more outreach with similar efficiencies or flow directly to the bottom line. Yet the most salient fact in accepting the ascendency of the Relationship Era paradigm has not to do with its benefits so much as its inevitability. The universe has made that decision for you.

There are four forces at work, converging momentously to dictate your future:

1. The ongoing collapse of mass media and the corresponding loss of advertising reach and efficiency have turned the economics of marketing upside down. The cost of reaching consumers with advertising messages and promotional offers is rising unsustainably, even as consumer tolerance for such messaging declines. In the meantime . . .

2. . . . the Internet has torn down the ramparts separating the corridors of business power from the teeming hordes. Once, corporations and brands could operate behind nearly impregnable fortifications. Now there is hardly an event that takes place—especially an ugly one—that doesn't become exposed to one and all, immediately and in perpetuity. Whereupon . . .

3. . . . thanks to the rise of social media, the news becomes conversational currency worldwide. And all of this has happened at a moment in time when . . .

4. . . . the public has decided that it cares not only about goods and services but about the values and conduct of the providers. Trust, at least according to survey data we shall explore, now frequently trumps even quality and price.

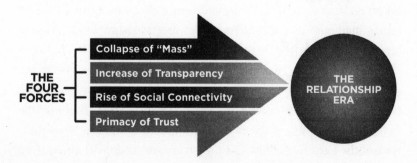

This unprecedented disruption in the status quo has left brands an apparent choice between two evils: continue to squeeze costs out of their budgets at the expense of the media and ad agencies living in the same ecosystem, a choice doomed by the law of diminishing returns, or dive headlong into social media, where "Likes" stand in for transactions, and where the huge audiences that have been so basic to mass marketing for centuries are seemingly impossible to attain.

In fact, though, that is not the choice at all. There is a third way—a human way—that happily converges with present reality. Now marketers can and must define their brands not by the ads, press releases, slogans, coupons, sponsorships and even product offerings but by their core purpose. Once defined and internalized, this single *raison d'être* will inform all interactions with customers, employees, shareholders, distributors, the trade, suppliers, neighbors, governments and the press—representing not some contrived "image making" but a starting point for ongoing relationships. These relationships manifest themselves face-to-face, in traditional communications channels, in the crucible of third-party word of mouth and ever more vastly online—where opportunities to meet and greet are endless. What flows from that commitment is the steady building of trust and fellowship, which may sound like Boy Scout pieties but that also build lifetime customer value, lower promotional costs and enhance share price.

It isn't hard to adapt to the Relationship Era. You needn't exactly forswear the hallowed Four Ps of marketing—product, promotion, price and place—but you must complement them with the Relationship Era's Three Cs: credibility, care and congruency. Does the brand engender public trust by delivering on its promises? Does it understand consumer needs and seek to fulfill them? Does its every action resonate with deeply held values?

As we shall see, the last of the Three Cs—congruency—is the one that has upset the assumptions of the traditional, transaction-centric marketing model. Up to this point, it was all about the goods. You were fine if you had the goods. Now there are new questions to be answered: How did the goods get there? Who benefited and who was harmed? And who, acting in the brand's name, has inspired me or disappointed me? Yes, the running shoes or light bulb or aisle seat is just fine, but excuse me, *Who are you?* As Bank of America, Nike, General Electric and even the vaunted Apple (all companies we will discuss in time) have belatedly discovered, those questions have changed everything. And if your answers fall short, you are very likely screwed. Admit it or not, like it or not, embrace it or not, exploit it or not, your business destiny is not in your hands. It is the hands of seven billion others. This would be a fine time, therefore, for a joining of hands.

For those who have spent careers trying to define their brands with ad slogans and bombast, such a proposition may seem absurd. "Hold *hands?* Why not just toss flower petals?" But even the most entrenched defender of the status quo recognizes that something has changed. The public is already constantly evaluating the brand and comparing notes on Facebook, Yelp and Tumblr. Their friendship, their ideas, their loyalty, their passions, their labor, their evangelism and not incidentally their business hang in the balance. Such goodwill represents incalculable value. Their indifference, distrust and, worst of all, hostility, represent incalculable liability. The question is, Absent now the ability to mesmerize the public on a mass scale, how can you be on the right side of all this teeming humanity?

Step-by-Step

In all humility, we believe we have the answer.

Can't Buy Me Like will offer a unique template for shifting from the rapidly deteriorating Consumer Era of mass marketing to the rapidly emerging Relationship Era—a transition that has stymied the most sophisticated marketers in the world.

Can't Buy Me Like will outline precisely—not in vague generalizations but *precisely*—how businesses can, and must, fundamentally change their relationships with customers, employees, suppliers, investors and all stakeholders, but only after first articulating for themselves exactly why they are in business in the first place.

Can't Buy Me Like will offer data and case histories demonstrating that the answer to the above question is not simply "To make a profit." Profit is the *consequence* of understanding your reason for being—your core purpose—and we have the growth stories to prove it.

Finally, *Can't Buy Me Like* will direct you safely away from some of the most common marketing malpractices emerging in the digital world. Your colleagues and competitors are doing some mighty foolish things out there. We will show you how not to do the same.

Please note: While the occasion for this book is a historic inflection point, the principles we discuss here are not fundamentally about the digital revolution, social media or technology any more than capitalism is fundamentally about the steam engine. We believe that cultivating relationships—versus unilaterally promulgating messages of seduction and persuasion—would have been a superior way of doing business in 1953, or 1983, as well as 2013. But we are not in 1953, and the option has been taken away from you.

Can't Buy Me Like begins wide to establish context and principles, and then progressively narrows. Our work begins with a survey of the chaotic status quo, a media and marketing symbiosis being pried apart by the forces of digital revolution. There we demonstrate that business as usual is not a sustainable option. From there we move on to the currency of commerce, trust and the new reality, the Relationship Era in which all institutions have suddenly found themselves whether they choose to accept it or not. Fortunately, as we shall demonstrate, new consumer mentalities have further unleashed the power of social connectivity to redefine—and supercharge—interaction between companies and citizens. Much of those interactions will hinge on shared interests, values and goals, none of which can be shared unless brands themselves embrace interests, values and goals beyond selling more freight cars full of YouNameIt. Thus we address the central requirement for all institutions in the Relationship Era to define and internalize a central purpose that influences all activities, internal and external, with all stakeholders.

On this subject we take up the case histories of Patagonia, Krispy Kreme, Secret, Zappos, Panera, Louisville Slugger, Kotex, Seventh

Generation, Method, World Vision, Sovereign Bank and others. These brands don't have customers so much as they have members, and they are your new role models.

These are feel-good sagas, but are we simply dispensing sermons, or pep talks or motivational speeches that send fired-up salespeople out of the hotel ballroom ready to take on the world, only to enter the parking lot and the uninspiring bullshit of day-to-day business reality? No. On the contrary, we demonstrate that Relationship Era thinking alone offers a sustainable means of achieving consumer trust, satisfaction, loyalty, labor, intellectual capital and brand ubiquity. Our Brand Sustainability Map, introduced in Chapter 2, is a visualization of the relationship—and asset value—of trust and success.

Having established that defining relationship of the Relationship Era, we will enumerate the differences between doing business in the Relationship Era *vis-á-vis* the waning Consumer Era. Then we offer "the Shift": a series of internal protocols for managing the transition, all the while dismissing the common objection that we are "changing the engines in midair." (As you shall see, it's a terrible analogy.) Nonetheless, that Shift implies a major philosophical and organizational reevaluation, flowing from which will be a major change in the way your brand engages with the world.

Fear not, however. We do not leave you dangling with a what but not a how. We break down a number of specific tactics for the heavy-duty "relating" we prescribe. This advice will range from understanding the significance and dynamics of the simple Facebook "Like" to the methodical leveraging of your stakeholder communities to gain more influence than you ever had from the media you've been paying through the teeth for through your entire careers. Or, put another way: It's better to be admired than ad mired.

It's better to be admired than ad mired.

New-ish and Improved

Loyalty. Evangelism. Purpose. You've heard these terms before. Likewise, perhaps you've noticed that none of those converging four forces from the above chart is, in and of itself, breaking news. After years of encroaching chaos, it is finally lost on nobody that the dynamics of business have gone haywire. Every CMO on earth has stood at a lectern before a nervous audience somewhere and mouthed the truism, "The consumer is in control." What has gone unsaid, and largely unnoticed, is the need not for incremental adjustment but radical transformation—a shift in marketing practices, yes, but more important a shift in mentality incorporating the well-documented observations and research of scholars and business leaders at least as capable as us. We have taken, as it were, "prior art" in social science and business, incorporated our own thinking, proprietary data and substantial experience and fashioned a working prototype for the modern consumer marketer. Our immodest goal is to be not merely financially, but something approaching spiritually, transformative.

A fair question at this stage might be, "Why should I listen to you about any of this, especially when you're talking about transforming my spirit? I have clergymen for that, plus, you know, Deepak Chopra." Well, in all humility, you should listen because we have climbed the mountain. We've spent many years exploring these concepts and seen them play out in the real world. We've seen how human beings respond. And, from entirely different starting points, we've made understanding the Relationship Era our life's work. Doug Levy is the founder and CEO of MEplusYOU, a strategic and creative agency based in Dallas and with offices in New York. There is plenty of dope on both of us in the authors' notes at the end of this book, but for now suffice it to say Doug is an active leader in the Conscious Capitalism movement and with his partners has gradually pioneered Relationship Era principles over more than a decade for marketers including, but by no means limited to, Procter & Gamble, TLC Laser Eye Centers, Coca-Cola, Louisville Slugger,

Pfizer, General Mills, and Samsung. Bob Garfield is a journalist and consultant whose Web site bio bashfully introduces "the most prominent commentator and analyst of advertising and marketing who has ever lived." Famous for a quarter century of ad criticism, he is also the author of books and articles that as early as 2005 foretold the "chaos scenario" now bedeviling marketers around the globe. He's also responsible for "Listenomics," a 2005 essay predicting and prescribing a rise in data mining and social listening. At the time, the entrenched powers largely rolled their eyes. Now the same people pay Bob obscene sums to help forge a path out of chaos. This book, synthesizing Bob's pragmatism and Doug's evangelism and experience, maps that path.

As such, *Can't Buy Me Like* is a bit of a manual and a bit of a manifesto. Mainly, though, it is a whole new way of imagining business and your role within it. Fueled by nothing less primal than human nature, it will enable a sustainable future for your enterprise, and, not incidentally, make you feel good about what you do each day. No longer will you drag your sorry ass out of bed in the morning to go sell stuff to people. You will wake up feeling connected, driven, and meaningful. In the end, what *Can't Buy Me Like* offers is uplift—for your business, for your stakeholders and for you.

1

GOOD-BYE TO ALL THAT

Every farewell combines loss and new freedom.

—MASON COOLEY

It used to be so easy. In the early days of advertising's creative revolution, George Lois, the profane ad man and sultan of blunt, used to win clients by telling them, "I'm gonna make you famous."

He was not lying. Once upon a time, you could actually advertise your way into the nation's consciousness, and thereupon into its pocketbook. It was just a question of buying space and gross ratings points. CBS and *Life* magazine did the rest. Yet little did George know that in historical terms, he was making his promise at the tail end of a mass-marketing epoch spanning more than three centuries.

It all began in seventeenth-century Holland and England, and remained more or less consistent for three hundred years. First came what we call the Product Era, defined by focus on the intrinsic—or allegedly intrinsic—qualities of the product or service. We chortle at the naiveté of ad copy dating to 1659: "*PANACEA*, or the Universal Medicine: Being A DISCOVERY of the WonderfullVertues OF Tobacco Taken in a Pipe."

Ha ha. How simplistic and hyperbolic! Except that by the mid-twentieth century, not much had changed. Advertising was *still* simplistic and hyperbolic, featuring the relentless extolling of product attributes real or imagined. Lucky Strike cigarettes preemptively claimed an industry-standard heating process as a unique selling proposition: "It's toasted!" Brylcreem claimed, snappily, "A little dab'll do ya!" And, let us not forget, "Everything's better with Blue Bonnet on it!" (In point of fact, not everything *was* better with Blue Bonnet on it, and we ask you to hold that thought.) The Product Era took America from Plymouth Rock to the Vietnam War in the company of Wonderfull Vertues.

The second, decidedly briefer stage of that epoch—from about 1965 to roughly five minutes ago—was the Consumer Era. This was characterized by a shift from advertising and marketing focused on the product to getting into the head and heart of the consumer. A fine example is MasterCard's "Priceless" campaign. The quintessential example is Nike's "Just Do It."

The Consumer Era cleaved to a four-step process: (1) ascertain through research what the public desires; (2) offer it; (3) create advertising designed to seduce, impress, entertain or flatter the target audience; and (4) place that advertising in media favored by the target.

Why not? Where's the flaw in selling people what they wish to have by reaching them with messages they relate to in the places they like to be? Thinking of others . . . isn't that what we're supposed to do? Companies such as Procter & Gamble, McDonald's, Toyota, Sears, Kellogg's and a few thousand others amassed vast fortunes with the simple strategy of giving people what they wanted. Yet, for three reasons, those universal marketing practices must be discarded. For starters, there is the toll of chaos.

Apocalypse Now

It begins with the collapse of mass media and mass marketing amid the havoc of digital revolution. This chaos has risen in the wake of the digital revolution. Enormous barriers of entry—the cost of a movie studio, or of printing presses and trucks, or of broadcast towers and transmitters—up to this point were surmountable only by a handful of heavily capitalized oligarchs. Now the cost of entry into film, publishing or videocasting is approximately the cost of an iPhone. The consequent glut has rendered those capital-intensive platforms no longer scarce and thus destroyed the revenue models of an entire sector of the economy.

On April 9, 1979, when the population of the United States was 29 percent smaller than it is today, a single episode of *All in the Family* entertained more than 40 million Americans.[1] On April 9, 2012, in the last hour of prime time, the top five English-language broadcast networks *together* commanded an audience of 29.7 million viewers.[2] Furthermore, because 40 percent of U.S. households have DVRs,[3] and because at least 50 percent of those with DVRs (depending on which study you believe; a 2011 *TV Guide* survey put the percentage at 96!) use them to skip past commercials,[4] the effective reach of a prime-time ad roadblocked against all five networks is reduced, on average, to no more than 20 million sets of eyeballs. Oh, no doubt, many of the other 295 million Americans are glued to their sets, but their attention is divided among 1,000 cable channels, Hulu, YouTube, Netflix and you name it. This is fragmentation, the enemy of mass.

In the same year that Archie and Edith Bunker so successfully hogged the airwaves, daily newspaper circulation was 62.2 million.[5] By 2011 (the last year for which statistics are available), it had dropped 29 percent to 44.4 million.[6] In the past fifteen years, overall ad revenue for print editions has declined by two-thirds—mainly because the classified-ad money machine has been plundered by craigslist, Monster.com, Autotrader.com and the like. And on the subject of plunder, we need hardly recount the pillaging of the record industry by iTunes—except to add that the $8.6 billion generated by iTunes and its like in 2012[7] represents no more than 5 percent of global downloads. The other 95 percent—or $173 billion worth—are simply pirated.[8]

The toll of the digital revolution does not end there. Magazines have been devastated; ad pages are down 42 percent since the year 2000 and ad revenue has dropped $5 billion since 2007.[9] Hollywood has been devastated; in 2011, the number of box office admissions was the lowest since 1995[10] and the likes of Netflix—not to mention BitTorrent—are poised to inflict more damage still. Commercial radio has been devastated, as literally half the teen/young-adult audience fled to digital devices over the past decade. Cable television is about to be devastated, once people figure out they can use their cables to pipe in only broadband, giving them free access to most of the content Comcast, Time-Warner, Cox and others are gouging them for every month in subscribers' fees. Imran Khan, an Internet analyst for Credit Suisse, says that 28 percent of cable subscribers expressed a willingness to cancel cable in favor of Boxee, Hulu, Netflix, and YouTube et al.[11] According to Nielsen, 4.5 percent of U.S. households have broadband but no cable subscription[12]—what *Wired* magazine calls "A State of Nirvana"—and that percentage is trending rapidly upward. Traditional book publishing, under siege from e-books and self-publishing and Amazon.com in general, is in the middle of a precipitous plunge; in 2011, for the first time, sales of e-books exceeded both hardcover and paperbacks.[13] The particular title you are reading happens to have been published by an old-line New York publisher. Enjoy the experience; it will be among your last.

So let us turn now to the Internet, which was to be the great salvation for advertisers, who could fulfill their long-held dream of precise targeting, based on the vast troves of data left behind wittingly and unwittingly by all of us as we surf the Web. Alas, privacy concerns have effectively denied marketers access to much of that data, lest Congress or regulators intervene, which, inevitably, they will anyway. But never mind that; it's practically a side issue. Recall that fragmentation, by definition, is the enemy of mass. Well, the Internet is not merely fragmented; it is hyperfragmented, verging on infinitely fragmented. Of the many hundreds of millions of Web sites, only a few have a large reach and fewer still are profitable. At least 99 percent never will be.

Sure, we are up to our necks in utility and content, much of it extraordinarily popular, but most of it is bankrolled by venture capital and the free labor of the multitudes. Alas, the virtually endless supply of online content has created a virtually endless supply of advertising inventory, which, by the law of supply and demand, inevitably drives prices down, down, down. Now do the math: An infinitesimally low CPM × small number of total eyeballs = a paltry revenue stream. There are approximately 350 million Web sites in the world. Not counting e-commerce sites, a few *thousand* Web publishers are significantly profitable. And most of them publish porn.

Then, to add grievous insult to mortal injury, no less than with TV, the very digital tools that have so undermined the economics of big media also render most online advertising utterly avoidable. Spam filters. Targeting opt-outs. Not to mention display-ad opt-outs, also known as free will. Ever clicked on a banner ad? No, of course you haven't.

As we like to say, with apologies to the 1960s, "The Revolution will not be monetized."

It is a confounding paradox: an economic revolution that in one critical aspect takes us backward.

This is bad for publishers and crippling for Consumer Era marketers. It is a confounding paradox: an economic revolution that in one critical aspect takes us backward. While digital tools have taken the power of the heavily capitalized few and distributed it to the many, they have also nearly obliterated *anybody*'s capacity to reach the many in one fell swoop. The Industrial Revolution was revolutionary because it created efficiency through scale. The Digital Revolution, by contrast, has decimated scale.

You'll Wonder Where Your Money Went

So, yes, upheaval is violently altering the landscape. A second factor is ecology. Think of the marketing environment like the planetary environment. In the Consumer Era, business won customers by constantly, expensively burning fuel. That fuel was advertising. Drill, drill, drill. Burn, burn, burn. Sell, sell, sell. Advertising and promotion were maddeningly transitory, a vast expense yielding very little equity. Buy advertising and, lo and behold, sales went up. Stop advertising and, oops, sales went down. Period. Once upon a time, the leading toothpaste brand in the United States was Pepsodent. ("You'll wonder where the yellow went when you brush your teeth with Pepsodent!") Now, long since unsupported by advertising, it languishes in tenth place with 1 percent share of the market.[14]

One of our favorite examples of this phenomenon, because unlike many marketing cases it is unclouded by mitigating variables, involves Colorado tourism. Back in the early 1990s, the state spent unextravagantly, but it spent wisely. Introducing a modest $12 million a year ad campaign, Colorado quickly catapulted from fourteenth to first among states as a summer resort destination. But when a tax revolt put the state's .2 percent (!) tourism tax up for referendum, the measure was soundly defeated and the $12 million budget was slightly reduced. To be specific, it was reduced to $0. Thereupon, within one year, Colorado's tourism ranking plummeted to seventeenth place. Within two years, it had lost 30 percent of market share, and an estimated $1.4 billion to its economy annually.[15]

This nightmarish anecdote speaks eloquently to the power of advertising. It speaks even more eloquently to the limits of advertising. Once the fuel valves were shut off, the engine stopped working. In ecological terms, marketing's effects were unsustainable. And now, amid the collapse of mass, the fuel itself is too expensive to produce. So now what? The future requires a sustainable alternative.

None of the foregoing is to suggest we wish to belittle advertising. On the contrary, we have made the study and practice the center of our intellectual pursuits, not to mention our livelihoods, for most of our careers. Plus, come on, the *Energizer bunny*! Volkswagen in the 1960s. George Lois's "I want my Maypo!" The Etrade baby. "Where's the Beef?" Apple's "1984." Absolut. "Diamonds are forever." The Marlboro man. What's not to like?

All right. Don't answer that question. We are well aware that the most effective ad campaign in history led to many cancer deaths, and, of course, that Madison Avenue—a la Blue Bonnet—frequently traded in casual lies. But permit us to turn momentarily to one of our most cherished sources of thinking on the industry, quoted here from his 2003 manifesto *And Now a Few Words from Me*:

> First of all, advertising works. Even bad advertising works in the rudimentary role of reinforcing a brand name and conveying the presumption of quality and substance conferred by the mere existence of national advertising. Furthermore, much advertising is simply brilliant, building brands, cultivating markets, and creating wealth that not only serves this country's economy, but that of the entire world.[16]

That Bob Garfield! We just can't get enough of him. The point is, though, that we harbor no animus toward the methods of the past; they have served well. And advertising will not disappear, nor should it. It's just that advertising's primacy in the commercial ecosystem is coming rapidly to an end. And if you don't take our word for it, perhaps you'll believe the biggest advertiser in the world, Robert A. McDonald, chairman and CEO of Procter & Gamble. In 2012 McDonald, he of the $10 billion ad budget, explained a reduction in paid media spending to investment analysts:

> We're quickly moving more and more of our businesses into digital. And in that space, there are lots of different avenues available. In the digital space, with things like Facebook and Google and others, we find that the return on investment of the advertising, when properly designed, when the big idea is there, can be

much more efficient. One example is our Old Spice campaign, where we had 1.8 billion free impressions and there are many other examples I can cite from all over the world.[17]

We can, too. In June 2012, at the Cannes International Festival of Creativity, we ran into Joel Ewanick, who at the time was CMO of General Motors. He had just come through two p.r. firestorms, one by canceling a $10 million ad buy on Facebook, on effectiveness grounds, and the other by pulling Chevy out of the Super Bowl. The latter move led to speculation about his competence, and his sanity—but he just shrugged off the criticism.

"Every single line in our budget is going to be reevaluated," he explained. "There are no sacred cows, including the NFL and Major League Baseball." Yikes, so much for "Baseball, hot dogs, apple pie and Chevrolet." More to the point, so much for the status quo. Sixty years of conventional wisdom certainly didn't influence the 2011 introduction of the Chevy Sonic subcompact.

"You know," he said, "we did five months of launch [initiatives in social media] before we ran a single TV ad—and it's the best-selling car in its category. If you were to ask me a year and a half ago whether you could launch a car without TV, I'd have said 'No way.'"

Well . . . way.

Who Is This Person the Supreme Court Says You Are?

As we have seen, resource management and the disintegration of mass alone argue against the status quo. But put them aside, because there is a third reason the sun is setting on the Consumer Era. It was, arguably, *always* a flawed way of doing business. The magnificent symbiosis of mass advertising and mass media to power mass manufacturing and mass distribution may have distracted us all from the inherent weakness in the system—namely, that in both the Product Era and the Consumer Era, businesses were slaves to externalities: consumer desires (actual and assumed), the competition's activities and the oppressive demands of the capital markets. Businesses learned to react quickly to every twitch in the marketplace, and in so doing, we believe, lost their way.

It is better first to look inward than to define your business by your public's often fickle and shortsighted tastes.

Counterintuitive as it may seem, and to be fleshed out in great detail presently, a pillar of the Relationship Era is that it is better first to look inward than to define your business by your public's often fickle and shortsighted tastes. Please note that in 1885, what the public wanted was more comfortable horse-drawn carriages. Try as we might, too, we cannot recall any significant agitation twenty years ago for a $4 cup of coffee. And, as Steve Jobs so accurately and arrogantly observed in explaining why there was no market research done in the development of the iPad, "It's not the consumer's job to know what they want."[18] George Bernard Shaw made the same point less obnoxiously: "The reasonable man," he wrote, "adapts himself to the world; the unreasonable one persists in trying to adapt the world to himself. Therefore all progress depends on the unreasonable man."[19] And then there was Polonius, who, for a fictional character, was extremely wise and perspicacious. Above all, he counseled his son Laertes as he sent the lad off to England, "To thine own self be true."

Now this gets into awkward territory for us, as the idea of internalizing unshakeable core principles may seem superficially to clash with the notion of collaborating and communicating with and above all listening to your customers and other stakeholders. It might seem hypocritical for the loud proponents of "Listenomics," such as ourselves, to imply that the listening should apply not to the outside world but to the voices in one's head. Come to think of it, that sounds not merely hypocritical but schizophrenic. But, in point of fact, as you shall see in subsequent chapters, we do not advocate authoritarianism or even benign Jobsian despotism. We by all means believe that Listenomics should inform every aspect of business—so long as the *first* voice listened to is the collective conscience of the enterprise. Because genuine relationships are built on equality, not subservience.

Genuine relationships are built on equality, not subservience.

Surely, people wish to be listened to. They want attention and fairness and honesty and empathy and respect. But there is no evidence, nor has there ever been outside of electoral politics and entertainment, that humans wish to be pandered to. Mutual respect is not fostered by sycophancy or servility. You know the awkward sensation of being waited on, with excessive deference, by a waiter or resort employee? You know how, especially in a third-world destination, a subtext of intense resentment emerges unconcealed by the hyperpoliteness and big smile? Businesses that prostrate themselves before customers at the expense of their own core vision, to say nothing of their dignity, evince no respect and therefore engender none. On the contrary, citizens the world over regard business as cynical because for centuries businesses have behaved cynically. Or, simply put: People who patronize you do not wish to be patronized themselves.

Simply put: People who patronize you do not wish to be patronized themselves.

The Relationship Era, we are happy to report, favors brands and individuals comfortable in their own skin.

2

THE RELATIONSHIP ERA

Connection is why we're here. It gives purpose and
meaning to our lives.

—BRENÉ BROWN, social scientist and author

Consider this simple experiment:

Type "I love Apple" into your search bar. You will get 3.27 million hits. If you type "I love Starbucks," 2.7 million hits. Zappos: 1.19 million.

And "I love Citibank"? You get 21,100. AT&T Wireless: 7,890. Exxon: 4,730. Dow Chemical: 3. Out of 7 billion human beings, 3! Just to put that into context: If you type "I love Satan," you get 293,000 hits. Now consider this: Citibank, AT&T Wireless, ExxonMobil and Dow among them spend $2 billion a year on advertising. Money, it turns out, really can't buy you love. It can't even buy you like.

The methodology here may not be especially rigorous, but the results dramatize three immutable facts of contemporary marketing life:

1. Millions of people will, of their own volition, announce to the world their affection for a brand. Not for a person, not for an

artwork, not for a dessert but for a good or service. Congratulations. People care about you.

2. Your brand is inextricably entwined in such relationships. If you were to type in "I *hate* Exxon," you'd get 2.16 *million* hits—not counting the "I hate ExxonMobil" Facebook page. People are decreasingly listening to your messages, but that hasn't stopped them from thinking about you and talking about you. And each of those expressions of like, dislike, ardor or disgust has an exponent attached to it, reflecting the outward ripples of social interaction.

3. What used to happen in the privacy of your own boardroom, plants and C-suite is now extremely public and common currency on the Internet. People in glass houses shouldn't do anything illegal, embarrassing, hypocritical, offensive, tasteless, vulgar, excessively greedy or otherwise incorrect—especially when getting caught being honorable and constructive has such benefits. Perhaps by coincidence, but most likely not, this sudden vast availability of information corresponds with a societal megatrend of judging institutions not only on their offerings but on their conduct. Thus, for the first time in commercial history, there is not just moral value but asset value in being a mensch.

This is the Relationship Era, the first period of modern commerce when your success or failure depends not on what you say, nor even on what you produce, but increasingly on who you are. And it isn't hard to discover who you are. Just Google yourself. Take your time. It's all there, in perpetuity.

Except for a handful of industrial juggernauts mainly removed from public view (including ExxonMobil, truth be told) doing business in the Relationship Era has many requirements. Ethical conduct. Seamless customer relations. Constant contact and cooperation with all stakeholders, including not just investors but also employees, suppliers, distributors and retailers, neighbors, governments and the society at large. It must be an all-pervasive imperative to earn the trust of all concerned—not as a means to gain advantage in a sale or negotiation but as an end in itself. We shall meditate on this subject in detail in the next chapter. Suffice for the moment to say that in bygone eras, trust was at best subsidiary to the all-pervasive focus on increased sales and market share. And in the current environment, the degree to which consumer trust influences purchasing decisions has never been higher and is clearly rising. Yet, paradoxically, trust and transactions are *independent variables*. Only when you view them as such can you fully understand their relationship in true brand sustainability, as we shall illustrate presently.

Meantime, let us nonetheless think about the value of trust relationships—versus the dependence on advertising and public relations to shape perceptions about a brand.

"It's always been about the individualized relationship," says Scott Olrich, CMO of Responsys, which provides relationship-based marketing software for some of the largest brands in the world. "A century or so back, the local corner shop lived or died based on the relationships they built. As new means of mass communication emerged, companies used their increased reach to try to advertise their way out of that responsibility. But today every aspect of a company's behavior is on public display. A relationship-first approach to every customer interaction has again become the imperative."

Dealing with this new reality requires an entirely new mentality across nearly all areas of an enterprise, in which every function of business embraces the Relationship Era—but in consumer interactions most of all. The behaviors associated with the Consumer Era nowadays seem cold-blooded and opportunistic, like a swinger on the prowl in a bar. The Relationship Era approach has more in common with romance, or, at least, a human connection.

Please don't misunderstand. We are well aware that there is nothing new, in and of itself, about relationships with customers. Every salesperson who ever took to the road, every rainmaker who paid for a round of golf, every beleaguered customer-service rep who tried to fix a problem before it escalated into service cancellation, every insurance agent who ever sent out holiday cards to policyholders, every airline that ever offered frequent-flier kickbacks to the businessperson flying on the company's dime, and surely every marketer who collected an e-mail address, or a postal address, or a phone number for subsequent up-sell has tried to foster a relationship.

Yeah, for the most part, that's not we're talking about. The relationships that businesses have mainly championed are those that are meant, one way or another, to grease the skids for a transaction. These relationships may be long lasting, and they may be mutually beneficial, but they are also superficial and opportunistic and sometimes even corrupt. Though they may seem to yield similar benefits, relationships forged as a tool of naked self-interest and those forged in the natural course of shared experience have vastly different qualities.

The poet and essayist W. H. Auden expressed this idea brilliantly. "Almost all of our relationships," he ruefully observed, "begin and most of them continue as forms of mutual exploitation, a mental or physical barter, to be terminated when one or both parties run out of goods." Auden wasn't speaking literally about business—barter was a metaphor—but he might as well have been. What Auden understood about human interactions is that value too often trumps values, that sharing too often means sharing the proceeds. Pure relationships are not transactional. This, however, is another paradox. While cozying up to prospects for the sake of doing business tends to be manipulative and inauthentic, business cannot flow sustainably without the establishment of connections that are genuine and mutually satisfying. More than that, by several key metrics with far more gravity than a Google search, sustainable relationships built on admiration and trust create significant financial premiums. They represent goodwill that can be isolated as a component of share value. They result in higher share prices. They reduce the cost of promotion, improving ROI and bottom-line performance. And, perhaps most of all, they create an opportunity for transcendence—the state of being so admired as to maintain an aura of magic.

The following is something you will be seeing quite a bit of. It is called the Brand Sustainability Map.

BRAND SUSTAINABILITY MAP

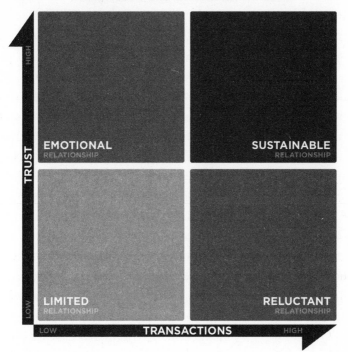

Researchers at MEplusYOU commissioned survey data on trust and plotted it against market share for leading consumer marketers.

Charting customer "trust" as the y-axis and transactions as the x-axis creates four quadrants. The lower left "limited" quadrant is the province of the losers: struggling brands with flat or declining sales that command little respect from the customer. To its right is the "reluctant" quadrant, brands that command little respect and generate little emotion, but whose price or competitive advantage trumps the consumer's misgivings. The upper left quadrant, "emotional," is the home of brands that maintain respect in spite of quality issues, limited distribution, high price or other competitive disadvantages. Finally there is Valhalla, the upper right quadrant called "sustainable." This is where you find the likes of Costco, Southwest Airlines, Apple and in the upperest right-handest corner, Amazon. Directly opposite, the lowerest left-handest corner of "limited"-ness, there lurks the axis of evil: Al Qaeda and American Airlines.

As we shall see in greater detail later, MEplusYOU's randomized surveys measured trust by polling on three separate criteria of consumer trust and transactions by asking about the frequency with which consumers choose a given brand within a given category. For a variety of reasons—chiefly nonuniformity in available sales and market-share data—this proved to be the most accurate metric of actual consumer behavior. For now, though, we ask you not to focus on methodology. Put aside, too, the notion of investing in the research required to definitively plot your brand on the grid. What matters most is the very *concept* of the Brand Sustainability Map. Once you accept what it reveals, you will most likely be able to intuit with some accuracy where your brand sits, and in which direction it is headed.

That exercise alone has triggered many a moment of clarity. To wit: In the Relationship Era, the big winners will be sustainable—where, not incidentally, habitués typically spend very little on advertising, because they don't need it. Indifference is expensive. Hostility is unaffordable. Trust is priceless.

Indifference is expensive. Hostility is unaffordable. Trust is priceless.

Some companies learn this by accident, happy or otherwise. Others have that understanding, you might say, baked in. One such is Panera Bread, the chain of almost 1,500 bakery-cafés in the "quick casual" restaurant segment. Panera's hallmarks are freshly baked bread, a healthy menu by chain-restaurant standards and welcoming service. The goal is to create what chairman and co-CEO Ron Shaich calls "positive energy" and personal touch. "That's our whole marketing effort," Shaich says. "It's fueling word of mouth. Marketing is simply amplification of the experience within. It's not like we are going to convince you that we are something that we are not."

What they are is successful and growing. Over the past fifteen years, the average Panera café has gone from $1.1 million in annual sales to $2.4 million. This is a reflection of total dedication to both customer experience and employee satisfaction, which are complementary for all the obvious reasons.

"I got a letter from a woman in Florida who was undergoing cancer chemotherapy," Shaich says. "And she came in without hair one day, one of our people reached over and gave her a hug and said 'Can we buy you lunch? We just want to be here in support of you.' And she was so moved by this, she wrote me. I mean this happens thousands of times when you can create that kind of space for people."

Such episodes, routine or not, are as affecting for employees as they are for clientele. Shaich says the ensuing company lore imbues the workplace with a sense of purpose.

"I would gather we have 60,000 people that work with us and are part of our company. I would guess that over the thirty years we've been at this, I probably have had hundreds of thousands who have come through as managers alone, and I can't tell you how many letters I get from people saying this was one of the most powerful experiences of their lives, being here.

"Profit is a byproduct. It's pretty clear to me, it's a byproduct of pleasing people and when you please people, they come back. And when they come back, they leave something." Yeah, including their money. Panera did $2 billion in 2012. Its stock chart looks like Mt. Rainier. Shares were selling for $15 in the year 2000.[1] Now they're at $169.[2]

Dialing for Scholars

We should say here that, in addition to staking no claim to the notion of relationships in marketing, equally we make no claim to first contemplating a Relationship Era. The ascendency of relationships in marketing has, in one form or another, been a subject of academic inquiry for at least thirty years, and the body of scholarship is substantial and growing. No bibliography is complete without the acknowledgment of such seminal works as Evert Gummesson's "Broadening and Specifying Relationship Marketing" (1994, *Asia-Australia Marketing Journal*), Jagdish Sheth and Atul Parvatiyar's "Relationship Marketing in Consumer Markets: Antecedents and Consequences" (1995, *Journal of the Academy of Marketing Sciences*), Tom Duncan and Sandra F. Moriarty's "A Communication-Based Marketing Model for Managing Relationships" (1998, *Journal of Marketing*), and Stephen L. Vargo and Robert F. Lusch's "Evolving to a New Dominant Logic for Marketing" (2004, *Journal of Marketing*).

Sheth and Parvatiyar were especially prescient. Having proposed nineteen discrete motivations for consumer loyalty, a number of which anticipate our conclusions, the authors commenced in 1995 to clairvoyantly describe the Relationship Era:

> In the future, marketer-initiated approaches to relationship marketing will become more prevalent and rise sharply. Technological advances are making it possible and affordable for marketers to engage in and maintain relationships with customers. Marketers now have the willingness and ability to engage in relational marketing. The willingness has come from the enlightened self-interest and understanding that customer retention is economically more advantageous than constantly seeking new customers. . . . There would also be some fundamental changes in marketing as a consequence of information technology. Technology would not only assist in relationship formation, it would also help in its enhancement, or even termination, of relationships. Through the use of information technology, consumers could enhance relationships with the marketing organization.[3]

Mind you, this was written before Twitter, before Facebook, before YouTube, before LinkedIn *before freakin' Google*. Whether the authors also bet on the crappy NY Giants to win Super Bowl XLVI, history does not record.

Another forward-looking vision has been espoused by UK scholars Michael John Harker of the University of Strathclyde, Glasgow,

Scotland, and John Egan of Middlesex University Business School, London, who in a pair of papers have observed that RM is, in practice, at best "bolted on" to the old paradigm. "Practitioners," they wrote in 2006, "appear to have borrowed the language without adopting the underlying values of relationship marketing." This behavior they speculate may emanate from fear of change, and even of obsolescence. "Perhaps if Relationship Marketing were to be widely adopted as the driving force behind organizational strategy there would be no need for the marketing function? Is it the marketer's relationships within the organization that require attention and repair?"[4]

Oh, snap! Take that, fearful hangers-on.

Butterfly Wings

For our part, we cannot sit and wait for the real world to catch up with the academy. Borrowing a buzzword or two is obviously not a substitute for new standards in investor relations, government relations, community relations, public relations, environmental conduct, business practices, legal and every single other activity and function of the enterprise. The proliferation of—and instant, perpetual access to—information from within the institution demands a total, irreversible embrace of Relationship Era practices across the board. Thus must organizations be entirely retooled to accommodate the Relationship Era. This question is no longer academic. It is a life or death proposition, right now—because the citizens formerly known as consumers now view institutions in their totality, and in a hyperlinked environment, everything you do is indeed linked in perpetuity. A butterfly flaps its gossamer wings in East Asia and the stock moves 1 1/8 in active trading.

As outlined in ensuing chapters, this means changing cultures of frontline employees—mainly by inspiring and empowering. That entails changing the mentality of management from the command-and-control status quo. That means listening deeply to stakeholders in search of converging interests and values. That means taking no relationship for granted, no matter how casual, because within each one resides the benefits of loyalty, labor, ingenuity and evangelism—not to mention entrée into their social, professional and family circles. It means attaining full understanding of social media, most especially Facebook and Twitter, not as channels for sending out ad messages but as virtual salons for sharing what humans share: observations, discoveries, ideas, concerns, interests, opportunities and just plain cool stuff of mutual relevance. In Chapter 10, you will see one such experiment conducted more or less before your eyes by an intrepid banking client in command of limited resources but in possession of tremendous vision.

The skeptical reader inquires: "How can sending out a few tweets mobilize a community of the faithful if $100 million in network TV buys can't even nudge market share fifty basis points? How can building relationships a handful at a time ever really amount to anything actionable?" The answer, it will not surprise you to hear, is there is no magic in Twitter or any other social-media platform. But there is a sort of magic in properly cultivating trust relationships—as documented in these pages by exactly the charts, graphs and data you expect. There will also be, of course, case histories, and we begin very briefly with three.

The first concerns the feminine hygiene brand Kotex. This is a category that, despite some courageous advertising ventured sporadically over the past decade, continues to be mired in euphemism and condescension—both of which reflect and perpetuate the sorry history of shame attached by society to menstruation. There are whole books to be written about the stigmatization of a basic reproductive function, an anatomical marvel reduced since biblical times to a matter of embarrassment and shame—especially for generation after generation of traumatized adolescents.

Kimberly-Clark and its agency Organic decided once and for all that Kotex would not only cease to be a part of such retrograde thinking but that Kotex above all was responsible for liberating its customers from the language and imagery of taboo. They did so by confronting the clichés of the genre head on: online video showed a super slow-mo image of a young woman twirling on the beach—the

universal feminine-care shorthand for freedom and "freshness"—
and called it "ridiculous." A Web site called U by Kotex solicited
ads spoofing the tropes of the genre; showed candid how-to demos
using actual products (vs. those labored visual analogies involving
blue liquid in a lab beaker), literally from the girl's point of view;
and encouraged girls to share their own experiences. Every element of the online effort, from the microsite to the Facebook page
to the online ads were designed to be interactive and shareable. The
education tab offered answers to user questions ("When I have my
period, it feels weird to go pee. Is this normal?") from an expert,
an ordinary mom of teenage girls and from a peer. Meantime, the
packages and products themselves eschewed the pale pastels of
modesty for a constellation of bold colors and patterns—and young
people were given a tool for creating designs of their own. More
than twenty thousand did just that. As Kimberly-Clark told visitors, "This is more than a Web site. This is a social movement
aimed at changing the conversation." The effort was called—ha ha
ha—"Break the Cycle."[5]

At this writing, according to Kimberly-Clark, more than four
million visitors have participated in some form of online activity.
Some three million have requested samples. First-year sales amounted
to $75 million and market share went from 4 percent in the first year
to 7.8 percent as of August 2012.

Life, Death and Trivia

While we're on the subject of teenage girls, a word about *la Quinceañera*.
In Mexico, as in much of Latin America, that is a central rite of passage for girls on their fifteenth birthday, the moment when they are
deemed to become women. It's like a bat mitzvah, only with more
tortillas.

In the fall of 2011, Microsoft wanted to celebrate the fifteenth
anniversary of Hotmail, but there was an obvious obstacle: Who
among Mexico's forty million Hotmail account holders would possibly care about the anniversary of an e-mail service? Especially

Hotmail, which throughout the world had been relegated to secondary status by Gmail. As Luis Gaitán, executive creative director at the agency DoubleYou explained to his client, "Guys, you've got to realize that Hotmail has become the biggest trash e-mail box on the internet."

This was not news to Microsoft, though it still reigned in Mexico, with twenty-four million unique users and 82 percent reach. To prevent the erosion seen in other countries, the brand wished to connect Hotmail somehow with Mexican culture and to establish an emotional connection, so that users could discover how much the service has improved. That got DoubleYou thinking about *la Quinceañera*. What if Microsoft asked account holders to submit e-mails that documented, or triggered, critical passages in *their* lives?

What happened next was eight thousand submissions of varying degrees of drama and poignancy.

"We had all kinds," says Gaitan. "There were a lot of stories about love. Others announced that they were pregnant." Job offers. University acceptance. An approval on a car loan.

To a professor: "From your mouth I learned that to live is not just to be breathing."

To an unrequited love interest: "If I could be your blood today, opt for the poison to take me to your heart."

And from an immigrant in Detroit to those at home: grim news of a rapidly spreading cancer. He did not get back to Mexico alive.

This national collaboration thus became an authentic celebration of what was deeply important to Hotmail and Hotmail users alike. It wasn't some self-aggrandizing and pointless brand anniversary but a national archeological expedition, unearthing not pre-Columbian pyramids but the epistolary artifacts of contemporary existence. Microsoft was spare with metrics in the wake of the campaign, but there's this curious fact: A book compiling the e-mails immediately sold out. And the agency offers this tidbit as evidence that the exercise cemented brand loyalty: Thousands of users reactivated dormant accounts to participate. Moreover, in Mexico, Hotmail remains *numero uno*.

So, yes, there are ample business stories to discuss in this dawning of the Relationship Era. For the moment, however, please consider one more anecdote about relationship building, one far afield of boardrooms and stock prices and market share and executive bonuses, yet still in all a revelation.

In early 2011, the Bob half of us spoke with a young woman named Mona Seif, who was a democracy activist at that moment in the thick of foment in Cairo's Tahrir Square. The conversation had turned to Twitter, whereupon Bob observed that the Arab Spring was a rather eloquent answer to those who dismiss Twitter as a tool of the self-indulgent blathering 140 characters at a time about the trivia of their lives. Curiously, Mona didn't bite.

"Yeah. I understand this criticism," she said, "because I've been getting it a lot from my friends, but the whole point is that engaging different people in bits of your life is really what makes it a powerful tool. Usually I use Twitter for really personal things, so I just share moments from my work or moments from my love life or I talk about my cats or my family. And it engages lots of different people, so when these people are following you and suddenly you are talking about a torture case, some of them might not usually be exposed to such cases. But because they are following me and there is an ongoing conversation between us, they would suddenly be engaged in this, as well."

So many marketers and other institutions believe that social media is just one maddeningly inefficient channel for selling their goods, services, politics or whatever. They see only the word *media* and ignore the word *social*. You cannot understand these technologies, much less benefit from them, if you do not first understand and internalize the idea that they are not about messaging; they are about relationships. Until you have established one, nobody much cares what you say. And you will never, ever be able to send a tweet like this:

Feb. 11: we got rid of Mubarak! Egypt won! #Jan25

3

TRUST ME

I never trust people's assertions, I always judge of them
by their actions.

—ANN RADCLIFFE, *1764*

Thinking of trust as just another mechanism for influencing
transactions, is like thinking about a child as just
another tax deduction.

—IAN WOLFMAN, CMO, MEPLUSYOU

The mother of all scandals it was not, but the summmertime 2012
calamity that befell Journatic is quite the cautionary tale.

Journatic (which is pronouced like "dramatic" but might better
be pronounced like "lunatic") had captured attention from a desperate newspaper industry by offering papers affordable, locally oriented content. Manna from heaven, in other words. The
inability—most likely the permanent inability—to produce such
content at low cost has combined with the loss of classified advertising revenue to propel the newspaper industry into a death spiral.
But Journatic had solutions: scraping data from public records for
quick 'n' dirty conversion to news stories, and outsourcing local reporting to writers who were reimbursed based not on the quality of
their output but the quantity. This formula seemed especially promising for so-called hyperlocal reporting, online neighborhood publi-
cations poised to tap vast pools of local advertising dollars. The

structural problem holding back hyperlocals has been that paying a salary and benefits to even a single local reporter, no matter how inexperienced and underpaid, can render such operations—which, by their nature, reach a limited audience—unaffordable.

So here was Journatic, offering actual reporting—however thin on context, nuance and local understanding—at a fraction of the typical cost. Unsurprisingly, the model intrigued some very big players, such as the *Houston Chronicle* and *San Francisco Chronicle*, both owned by Hearst. The faltering media giant Tribune Company not only purchased Journatic's service, it bought into the company.

"We're excited to partner with Journatic, both as an investor and as a customer," said Dan Kazan, Tribune's senior vice president of investments. "Journatic will expand Tribune's ability to deliver relevant hyperlocal content to our readers, and we believe that many other publishers and advertisers will benefit from its services as well."[1]

That was in April. In June it was revealed that Journatic outsourced, all right. It outsourced to the Philippines, where pieceworkers with dubious command of English, let alone journalism skills, were churning out filler for some of America's most venerable newspapers. Oh, and they were using fake bylines.[2] Oh, and some Journatic stories were created not through the miracle of data mining but through the miracle of plagiarism. Commotion ensued. The word *sweatshop* was invoked. Readers freaked. Customers fled.

But here's the part of the commotion that bears close scrutiny: In the middle of the July meltdown, Journatic editorial director Mike Fourcher resigned via a blog post that said, in effect, "I told you so." Scraping courthouse data to list transactions in real estate sections may work, he told his former employees and readers, but actual news can be mediated only via human beings with an understanding of the interests of the human beings at various stages of the transaction. The process requires, he wrote, "traditional bonds of trust."[3]

Ah. Trust. *That.* "The problem with Journatic," Fourcher said, "was focusing so much on cost that it failed to consider even the most basic prerequisites for trust internally, never mind the trust of people reading the newspapers.

"Even after the actual incident with fake bylines, I urged the founders to make policy changes, to establish a clear mission," the ex-editor declared. "The company has no written mission, has no written values. I encouraged them to do so explicitly and they chose not to."[4]

If Fourcher's narrative is to be believed, management chose wrong. By the time August arrived, fewer people trusted Journatic than could pronounce it. This was a company that had identified a gigantic marketplace and engineered a solution. It understood business needs. It found ready partners and customers. But it made three key mistakes: It believed it could cut corners without being detected, which is impossible in today's environment of Internet-imposed transparency; it neglected *human* needs and expectations at every level of the enterprise; and it forgot *why* journalism matters. Once upon a time, such a high-handed approach to business was altogether common. It is now altogether unsustainable. The dynamics of business have entirely changed.

Trust is now the basis for everything. But we must define our terms.

There Is Trust and There Is Trust

This was one of those indelible experiences that inform a man's impression of the world we live in. The scene was a lunch table at a Marina del Rey hotel meeting room. The occasion was a J.D. Power automotive marketing conference, the year 1990-something. There were ten people at the table eating chafing-dish salmon. One of them was one of your coauthors. Another was an extremely prosperous California car dealer. The subject of consumer trust had come up, whereupon the car dealer chimed right in. "I know just what you mean," he began.

We want people to feel at home in our stores. We want them to feel like they're among friends. If I see a lady who looks like she's worried about the process, I'll just have her into the office, just to talk. Not to sell, just to visit, to find out something about her, share something about us. It is so important to establish that trust. And then, once we've done that, we can really squeeze 'em!

Upon the realization that this lecture was being delivered in dead earnest, nine people were rendered speechless. The only response was the sound of cutlery madly clinking against hotel china. The guy's dumbfounded audience, most of whose members were in the car business themselves, could not tell if he was the most cynical man in their industry or merely the most oblivious. And surely they appreciated what this cardboard-cutout stereotype of a slick car salesman did not: that trust constructed as a means to a mercenary end is not trust at all.

Trust constructed as a means to a mercenary

end is not trust at all.

Actually, in a sense, the cynical car dealer wasn't wrong; for most of his business career, as long as the cars he sold weren't lemons— and the suckers never figured out they really didn't need the fabric protection, undercoating and supplemental warranty they were conned into buying—they most likely *did* trust their dealer and re-turned to be taken advantage of the next time. Alas, while this mini-tycoon was a pig, he wasn't an unusual pig. For centuries, ad-vertising and direct-selling techniques have been steadily abused by bad actors seeking to win transitory trust only to use it as a cudgel against the unsuspecting. Yes, the very confidence games employed by street grifters—subtle lies and misdirection—have also been em-ployed by major brands marketing food, financial services, energy, drugs and entertainment. (Weirdly, after political advertising, the most consistently dishonest category is Hollywood movies, which routinely misrepresent the source and substance of third-party reviews in their ads. Fortunately, the stakes there are low. When insurance companies fake empathy only to behave as predators when a claim is filed, tragedy is layered upon tragedy.) This sorry history, of course, has done nothing to raise the reputation of advertising itself. According to a 2012 Nielsen study of twenty-eight thousand respondents in fifty-six countries, trust in advertising—historically one of society's most suspect institutions—has somehow managed over the past three years to further plummet.[5]

That decline hasn't taken place in a vacuum.

Historical circumstances have converged to decimate the image-making power of advertising just as the Internet has given the public unprecedented levels of information about corporations and brands. According to same Nielsen survey, trust in TV, magazine and news-paper ads has plummeted an average of 23 percent over the past three years, while confidence in word-of-mouth, online reviews and other so-called earned media has grown to 92 percent.[6] Simultaneously, but probably not coincidentally, society has begun to judge our insti-tutions not merely by what they offer but by their conduct, their makeup, their motivations, their inner workings and even their inner selves. In short, people trust companies for the same reason they trust people. Institutions have joined the ranks of humanity.

Restoring faith in brands is so elemental, in fact, that we should be able to declare "be trustworthy" and call it a day. But *trust* turns out to be a more multifaceted and ambiguous word than meets the eye. On one end of the spectrum, there is the most rudimentary dimen-sion of confidence in a good or service: trusting that it will be accept-able and that the marketer will make things right if it fails to deliver. That is the baseline, implicit for any nationally advertised brand. It is one of the reasons virtually all advertising, however warily it is re-ceived by the public, nonetheless works: Because beyond awareness, information and brand personality, the very existence of the ads im-plies an acceptable minimum of quality, stability and integrity. That level of trust is not nothing but neither is it much to aspire to. "Prob-ably not a cheat" is not the most impressive recommendation.

Of course, it is better than the impression left by the establishment of trust followed by utter betrayal of trust, as described by our car-dealer friend. But in the Relationship Era, what constitutes trust has itself evolved from the confidence (however misplaced) that you wouldn't get screwed in a transaction. A famous ad jingle of the 1960s went "You can trust your car to the man who wears the star . . . the big, bright Texaco star!" Just try to imagine any oil company invoking the word *trust* in 2013. In boxing they'd call that "leading with your chin," because in the Relationship Era, trust has evolved. It is now the by-product of genuine commitment to genuinely mutual values and interests. And it is now central to purchase consideration.

This new reality is made evident by the longitudinal survey called the Edelman Trust Barometer.

As recently as 2006, Edelman Public Relations informs us, in answering what was the standard of trust, consumers most often cited "quality products and services." And why wouldn't they? Absent any notion of how the business went about its business, the basic fact of delivering on promises was sufficient to satisfy customers. If he could sell you gasoline for no more than the Mobil station caddy corner, and maybe change your muffler on short notice, you really could trust the man who wears the Texaco star. Historically speaking, if Maybelline said its mascara will make your lashes "long, longer, longest"—and it worked, and your eyes didn't swell shut, and the goo didn't clot or clump—nobody was going to lose faith in the brand. If East Coast poultry giant Perdue commanded a premium for its plump, yellow chicken breasts, and they indeed looked less pale in the meat case, and if they cooked up juicy and delicious, people would credit the snarly founder's claim, "It takes a tough man to make a tender chicken."[7] Once again, until very recently in the history of commerce, all you had to do was deliver the goods. No more.

City Hall Is Now a Soft Target

Nowadays, if you sell chicken, you are at pains to explain the conditions at the broiler house. In fact, each bird had better come with a medical chart. If you sell mascara, it had better not have been tested on bunny rabbits. Likewise, General Electric may build CT scanners that save the lives of smiling South Asian children, just like on TV, but the company still must answer for 1.3 million pounds of polychlorinated biphenyls dumped into the Hudson River over the course of thirty years. Nike can inspire millions the world over by embracing the grit, beauty, drama, virtuosity, personality and the self-actualization of sport, yet faces lingering suspicion and resentment over its dependence on contract sweatshops in East Asia through the 1990s. So sensitive is the public to corporate malfeasance that a three-store chain of Maryland pizzerias felt obliged to devote a portion of its menu to "About the coal we use" in the pizza ovens. Calm down, everybody: it's anthracite.

So if Coal Fire Pizza has to worry about backlash, imagine Rush Limbaugh's advertisers. In March 2012, when the right-wing blunderbuss called Georgetown University law student Sandra Fluke "a slut" and a "prostitute" for testifying before Congress in favor of government-subsidized contraception, citizens got to work boycotting Limbaugh's sponsors. This led to a rapid exodus, with Sears, JCPenney, Netflix, AOL and dozens of others tripping over one another to get out of the door.[8]

Once upon a time, of course, they could have waited for the tempest to blow over, its unfortunate associations papered over by feel-good advertising or diminished by consumer disengagement—disengagement due to both lack of information and a sense of helplessness in confronting large institutions. "You can't fight city hall," conventional wisdom for pretty much the whole of the twentieth century, is seldom ever uttered because it is no longer true. The Internet has provided the resources to know what The Man is up to and to very much take him on. Invested with such power, modern consumers care about and express themselves about issues that were nonissues for most of human existence—and they do so with unprecedented access to data, documents, journalism and to this point isolated uproars concerning virtually every activity undertaken by every company virtually everywhere in the world.

Even in China, despite extreme monitoring and censorship, microblog platforms have precipitated major scandals. In 2011, for instance, the Shuanghui Group's Shineway brand of pork products were revealed to have been processed from hogs fed with clenbuterol, an illegal additive that poisons humans.[9] When a derailment of the nation's new magnetic-levitation trains killed thirty-eight people and injured two hundred in the same year, the government ordered the media not to cover the accident, and the media obliged—but cell phone pictures from the scene spread in social media and soon revealed that the authorities had brought in earth-moving equipment to literally bury the evidence.[10] If there is nowhere to hide in China, it's folly to think you can operate under the radar here. You think you can protect secrets? Ask Brett Favre, Hall-of-Fame penis texter. Or ask the U.S. Department of State about Wikileaks. Heightened awareness combined with digital access has made the governments of the world, and the Fortune 1000, a Levittown of glass houses.

The apotheosis of technology-driven transparency is GoodGuide. Led by UC–Berkeley professor Dara O'Rourke, GoodGuide employs a team of chemists, toxicologists, nutritionists, sociologists, and life-cycle analysis experts to research and rate consumer products on health, environmental impact and on impact to society. To date it has rated upward of 175,000 toys, foods and packaged goods on a 1 to 10 scale. Consumers can search products at GoodGuide.com, or use a mobile app to scan products at retail. Then, in an instant, they can discover that Honest Tea is rated 8.6 overall, and Pepsi is rated 4.9.

What Time Is It? It's Chart Time!

It will come as little surprise, then, that by 2010, mere "quality" as a standard of brand confidence had dropped to number three in the Edelman Trust Barometer. Number one—with 83 percent citing it—was "transparent and honest practices."[11] Good conduct. Solid citizenship. Core values. The stuff of essential self. Scan the signage at the Occupy Wall Street encampments. Goldman Sachs takes a drubbing. Google, whose managers are very much in the despised 1 percent, somehow gets a pass.

Of course, how people represent themselves in surveys and rallies doesn't necessarily reflect how they behave in the real world. Nobody ever declares himself a racist. Surveys of media diets somehow reflect zero use of porn. This is what social scientists call the Attitude-Behavior Gap. So how to demonstrate that the public's stated preference for honesty and transparency squares with their actual choices in the marketplace? The answer, once again: the Brand Sustainability Map.

The brands inhabiting the upper right quadrant, please recall, enjoy lower promotional costs and higher lifetime customer value—because they have less churn than those below the grid's equator. The lower left corner is the province of the trust challenged, who must pay through the nose in advertising and promotion just to keep that nose above water. Mainly we will be showing single-category versions of the map—telecom, say, or fast food—but here's what the chart looks like with a whole assortment of actual brands plotted in:

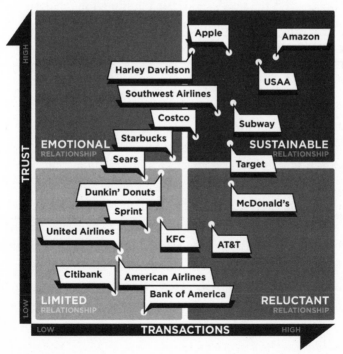

BRAND SUSTAINABILITY MAP

Yep, Costco, people trust you. Why, apart from basking in the glow of approval, does that matter? Because those whom we trust and adore we trust and adore *a lot*. That's simply human nature, and the benefit goes far beyond increased lifetime customer value. It creates the priceless effect of civilian advocacy. Social media have taken the stolid, dependable, venerable old tortoise—word of mouth—and transformed it into countless hares, multiplying like . . . well . . . like hares . . . and zipping around not just the salon and the saloon but also Facebook, Twitter and Yelp at the speed of "send." Yes, even as the digital revolution was undermining mass, it was supercharging human nature. The new challenge, according to David Rogers, executive director of the Center on Global Brand Leadership at Columbia Business School is "How do you as a marketer get the subset of the loyal customer who doesn't just buy your product again but goes out and writes those positive reviews? They share your links and retweet you on Twitter and post a photo of themselves with your product on Facebook and 'like' you on Facebook and generate all these network conversations." And in so doing, they change the shape—and the physics—of the traditional purchasing funnel. "Awareness, opinion, consideration, preference and purchase" have been supplemented, crucially, by "loyalty" and "advocacy."

The Three Cs of Trust

There is no such thing as a perpetual motion machine, but this gets close. The word-of-mouth effect creates a virtuous circle of trial, satisfaction and advocacy—a loyalty loop that functions most efficiently for the most admired brands. That is precisely what makes them sustainable. That is what drives their promotional costs down and their profits up. As we have learned from the piggish car dealer, though, there is trust and there is trust. For the purposes of measuring brand sustainability, MEplusYOU broke the concept down to three progressively complex components. They are as follows:

Credibility

This is a hoary concept in no way unique to the Relationship Era. It's simply the age-old imperative of delivering on promises. In fact, it is the beating heart of national brandedness: the presumption that at a minimum the marketer can be depended upon to meet the terms of the offer. A brand is itself essentially a proxy for that precise element of trust. If Hertz Number 1 Club gets you in and out in a hurry, they've once again maintained credibility. If the M&Ms melt in your hand, and not in your mouth . . . well, Houston, we have a problem.

Virtually all brands pay attention to credibility. They know they must deliver. But brands often think of credibility as *all* it takes to build trust, which is silly. Your lunch date could consistently be on time, and that's a whole lot better than getting stood up, but it alone doesn't create a very deep relationship. Your insurance broker will never, ever be late for lunch. This does not make him your friend.

Care

Through the whole of the Product Era and Consumer Era, marketers arguably cared about consumers. Indeed the essence of marketing was to divine the needs and desires of the target audience, then to fulfill them. But there are two problems with the term *target audience*: (1) "target" and (2) "audience." A target is a thing that is shot at, and an audience passively listens. Neither concept has a role in the Relationship Era. One of the hallmarks of Relationship Era thinking is the end of the adversarial "us" and "them" mentality,

with consumers, vendors or anyone else. Caring about consumers means actually caring about their lives and constructing your business to be as helpful as you can. And it means that, no less than the marketer, the buyer in every transaction should have succeeded.

Congruency

If the green movement, animal rights, Wikileaks, organic food and Occupy Wall Street tell us anything, it is that the public has more information about corporate activities than ever before and an ever-deeper interest in how big institutions behave. (Shortly we shall see how crucial reputation is to share price itself.) But it is not just conduct to which the public is attuned. People are increasingly reading the body language of corporations in search of the intangibles: beliefs, values, purpose. This demand for congruent values is the most difficult to measure, but also the most defining aspect of the Relationship Era. It is why the Edelman Trust Barometer has so changed over only three years. It is why individuals do not simply consume a brand but join it. It can also be why individuals resign their memberships. As we shall see, prospering in the Relationship Era hinges largely on how well you find common cause with individuals on the same wavelength.

Adding to the mounting evidence for the primacy of trust—and its catalytic role in the word-of-mouth ecosystem—was a 2011 study of content sharing, underwritten by the marketing department of the *New York Times*. It drew two central conclusions about how to become part of the conversation:

1. Appeal to consumers' motivation to connect with each other—not just with your brand.
2. Trust is the cost of entry for getting shared.[12]

Brand Power

Meantime, the value of relationship building can be demonstrated in other ways, too. For example, the marketing consultancy Core-Brand employs tracking studies of one thousand companies dating back more than twenty years to correlate brand reputation with asset value in a formulation it calls Brand Power.

Brand Power is ascertained by measuring "familiarity" and "favorability" via 10,000 phone surveys per year with VP-level managers and those higher up at Fortune 1000 companies.[13] Respondents are asked to rate other public companies based on investment potential, perceptions of management and, crucially, overall reputation. The scores are indexed for comparison on a 0 to 100 scale. In 2011, for instance, the average Brand Power value was 24. Apple was 74. GlaxoSmithKline—doing business among its own missteps in the scandal-plagued and widely loathed pharma category—was 17. Johnson & Johnson, despite a series of scandals, still scored a 75 but notably had squandered considerable reputation capital. In 2008, its Brand Power value was 84.

What does Brand Power mean, in dollars and cents? By overlaying financial performance metrics and brand communications expenditures you can derive the brand's value. Were you to divide the components of a company's stock performance, most of the pie would be wedges representing fundamentals: cash flow, profit, market share, dividend, price trajectory, cash on hand, plant and equipment and so on. But one wedge is attributable to unknown intangibles. Using regression analysis—assigning weights to the many variables affecting share price in thousands upon thousands of permutations—CoreBrand's statistical model deduces the size of the wedge attributable to brand equity. Brand Power is the reflection of the amount of brand equity relative to the company's overall market capitalization. In any given year, on average for the eight hundred companies studied, brand equity amounts to 5 to 7 percent of total equity value. For the strongest corporate brands, the wedge is worth 21 percent. In the fourth quarter of 2011, Apple's was 16 percent. Textron, the defense contractor that notoriously manufactures cluster bombs, rated 3 percent.

Perhaps the most poignant illustration of reputational power is the effect on Brand Power for a company in crisis. When Texaco was found to have engaged in widespread racial discrimination in the workplace, the $176 million in legal judgments[14] was a negligible drain on cash resources, but the negative publicity yielded plummeting brand favorability metrics and a corresponding pressure on stock price. It was five years before the favorability ratings and Wall Street equilibrium were restored. When Firestone tires were alleged to trigger rollovers in Ford SUVs, Firestone parent Bridgestone went into a reputational slump that lasted a decade.

CoreBrand historically has advised clients to influence the power of its corporate brand via the substance and sum of its advertising. However, troughs in reputation scores are typically tied to internal and external events—which means that corporate conduct directly affects stock price. It also suggests that enlightened, purpose-driven companies will be rewarded on Wall Street. (It also suggests that companies such as Procter & Gamble, which subordinate the corporate brand to their product brands, are leaving some share value on the table.)

What Brand Power, the Trust Barometer, the *New York Times* survey and especially the Brand Sustainability Map demonstrate is that trust is an indispensable asset in the Relationship Era. The rest of this book is devoted to demonstrating how to earn it. Let's begin, though, by explaining how not to:

1. Don't bother with window dressing. So many brands attempt to buy respect points—for instance, by linking themselves to unassailable causes such as sick kids as part of a promotion or a long-term "cause-marketing" strategy. This behavior is cynical and often sordid, exploiting other people's tragedy to purchase borrowed interest . . . not very different from 7-Eleven licensing *Iron Man* for a Slurpee copromotion. As Jeremy Heimans, CEO of the agency called Purpose, says, "The typical cause marketing is often very peripheral to the core business, very thin or very hollow: 'one dollar from every

purchase goes to the Save the Rainforest fund.' It's one step beyond 'We donate to the opera.'"

2. Don't pay lip service to CSR—corporate social responsibility— to inoculate yourself against charges of venality, environmental rape, offshore jobs, whatever. This is generally little more than p.r. gloss, a toothless "policy" to slap onto the annual report and forget about thereafter. All of which is both cynical and futile. Trust is an asset, not a commodity. It cannot be purchased. It must be earned.

Trust is an asset, not a commodity. It cannot be purchased. It must be earned.

---

3. Don't be like that venal car dealer, securing your trust only to immediately abuse it. So many marketers dangle one foot in the twenty-first century while putting all their weight on the other foot, firmly planted on top of the hard-sell's grave. Oh, they imagine themselves as modern practitioners making substantial investments of time and personnel in social media—whereupon they promptly squander the unprecedented potential of the online feedback loop by conducting themselves as aloofly in social media as they always have in paid media. Here is how one struggling fast-food chain has chosen to honor the individuals who honor the brand by following it on Twitter:

> KFC Colonel Everything's better with #bacon! Try a #KFC Cheesy Bacon Bowl for just $3.99 + tax. (Limited time at participating U.S. KFCs)

"You are our fan," KFC seems to be saying. "You are a member of our club! You are our friend! So, friend, we'll interrupt you as we always have with a sales pitch!" It's like being invited to another couple's house for dinner only to realize, over dessert, that you've been suckered into an Amway solicitation. Ugh. Cross them off the Christmas card list.

4. Don't be a scoundrel. Duh. Don't dump tons of toxic waste in the Hudson River. Don't dump tons of toxic assets in an offshore subsidiary. Don't hire child labor. Don't bribe officials of foreign governments. Don't bribe officials of domestic governments. Don't rely on fine print. Don't fly in on a private jet from your Palm Beach winter home to close down a plant. Don't cheat people out of their life savings. Don't get children addicted to carcinogens. Don't infringe on patents. Don't strong-arm retailers. Don't fix prices. Don't bully competitors. Don't evade taxes. Don't plunder the pension fund. Don't let your contractors and suppliers do anything you shouldn't do. Don't lie about your products. Don't lie about your financials. Don't lie about anything.

Those four "don'ts" constitute a pretty good start. But let's assume your particular enterprise engages in no such illegality, immorality, cruelty or just plain ruthless indifference to the welfare of the innocent. In a world that increasingly values values, "basically not sociopathic" is a good thing to be. It is not, however, the sort of quality that captures people's imagination. Here's a sentiment that has never been uttered: "I tell you, I really like Dan. He doesn't seem to be a repeat felon." But the following sentiment, phrased one way or another, surely has: "I really like that Dan. He's a straight shooter. He says what he means, he means what he says and he's got the courage of his convictions. The guy seems really comfortable with himself. He knows what is important, and he really seems to care. That Dan, quite a guy."

So, be Dan. Be straightforward. Exude confidence (but not arrogance) and decency. Care, deeply, about what you do and about all who are affected by it. Have a set of bedrock principles, but also a clear sense of purpose and understand that "maximizing shareholder value" doesn't qualify as a purpose. Mind you, as we have said and will say again, embracing the Relationship Era will indeed maximize shareholder value in the long run. But share price isn't why anyone buys your goods and services. It isn't why your assembly line workers or sales team or accounts payable staff work for you. It most certainly isn't why anyone wears your logo T-shirt or Likes you on Facebook or declares their enduring love in a blog post. Those are functions of affection and trust, neither of which are influenced by your balance sheet or quarterly earnings call. They are a function of what you intrinsically project. Not what you *say*. Not what you contrive as your slogan. What you *project*, like Dan, by all you do—and sometimes, of course, by what you don't do. And all of that begins with why you do it.

4

ON PURPOSE

Many men go fishing all of their lives without knowing
it is not fish they are after.

—HENRY DAVID THOREAU

For twenty-five years, United Airlines' theme has been *Rhapsody in Blue*, and no wonder. While George Gershwin's jazz-age masterpiece got a tepid reception back in the actual jazz age, it has since become a cherished part of the symphonic canon and a revered piece of Americana. It's dramatic, it's catchy, it's apropos of blue skies and it's—pay close attention here—utterly *uplifting*. It is simply difficult to imagine a musical theme better positioned to reshape public perception of United, which by 1987 had already made a mockery of its other long-standing advertising theme, "The Friendly Skies." Due to liquidity problems, volatile fuel costs, expensive mergers, labor friction and calcified management in general, United's skies were increasingly unfriendly. Its ad agency, Leo Burnett, alighted on Gershwin hoping that by waxing rhapsodic, and by sheer power of metaphor, they might lull the flying public into forgetting that the airline sucked. Better still they hoped the transcendence of the ad campaign would inspire employees to transcend their employer's growing crappiness to once again personify the joys and comforts of air travel.

For a solid quarter century Burnett and then successor ad agencies Fallon and McGarry Bowen kept it up, trying their damndest to imbue their client with a personality it did not possess. The TV commercials got beautifuller and beautifuller while the United experience got uglier and uglier. High fares and surcharges. Shrunken schedules. Surly, mistreated employees. Reduced services. No pillows. Pay-as-you-go food. Fees for ticket changes. Fees for bags. Fees for child escorts. Lost luggage. Long waits and a litany of petty humiliations—not the least of which was insolence in the face of its own ineptitude. That issue was dramatized memorably in 2009, when musician Dave Carroll of the Canadian band Sons of Maxwell, penned a little ditty about his personal United nightmare, videoed his rendition of it, and uploaded it to YouTube. We'll let the lyrics speak for themselves:

I flew United Airlines on my way to Nebraska
The plane departed Halifax, connecting in Chicago's "O'Hare."
While on the ground, a passenger said from the seat behind me,
"My God, they're throwing guitars out there"

The band and I exchanged a look, best described as terror
At the action on the tarmac, and knowing whose projectiles these
*   would be*
So before I left Chicago, I alerted three employees
Who showed complete indifference towards me

United . . . you broke my Taylor guitar
United . . . some big help you are

You broke it, you should fix it
You're liable, just admit it
I should've flown with someone else
Or gone by car . . . 'cause United breaks guitars.[1]

There's plenty more, documenting the whole sordid saga, but you get the idea. Strangely, while a quarter century and several billion-dollars worth of Gershwin didn't seem to capture the imagination of the flying public, Carroll's zero-dollars protest song immediately did. Because it rang all too true. "United Breaks Guitars" was viewed 150,000 times on the first day, on the way to 10 million views altogether.[2] Correlation isn't necessarily causation but in the aftermath United's market capitalization fell 10 percent.[3] In fulfill-ment of D. H. Lawrence's insight, truth had bested personality. And humanity had trampled billions of dollars of advertising ex-penditures into the ground. United hadn't much embraced relation-ships, but stood by helpless when the Relationship Era materialized before its horrified eyes. The question is, apart from the particulars of pissing off exactly the wrong passenger in particularly spectacular fashion, what was United's mistake? Was it simply devoting too little time and attention to its customers?

First Put On Your Own Mask . . .

The answer, oddly enough, is no. Oh, maybe in this instance they fell down on virtually every aspect of customer service imaginable, but in the larger sense United's mistake was that it neglected itself—its own core purpose, which, if we're not mistaken, was supposed to be making the skies friendly. Who knows . . . maybe that was just empty sloganeering, too, but considering they are a service-oriented company competing against other companies that offer essentially the same service, it surely should have been more than that. In the Relationship Era, the starting point is the brand. The brand must know and be true to its self before it presumes to interact with the outside world. As we shall soon see, marketers that thrive in the Relationship Era are clear on their purpose. A clear purpose defines what the brand or company stands for, beyond the financials, and inspires people not merely to patronize the brand, but to *join* it. Such brands (and other institutions) generate passion and loyalty, allowing them to be themselves instead of assuming a contrived advertising personality. Pretty girls don't have to slather themselves in makeup. And kind girls don't have to act cool.

Pretty girls don't have to slather themselves in makeup. And kind girls don't have to act cool.

People know who they are. And people know who *you* are. You are being evaluated not just for what you sell but by how you conduct yourself in the world—with consequences that flow directly to the bottom line. That truth was strikingly documented by Rajendra S. Sisodia, David B. Wolfe and Jagdish N. Sheth in their 2007 book *Firms of Endearment*, a study of what the authors call "stakeholder relationship management" or SRM. They selected thirty companies they deemed driven by purpose, as opposed to slavish devotion to quarterly earnings, and showed how they built up shareholder value by, as paradoxical as it may seem, *not* obsessing on shareholders. Among those selected were Honda, Trader Joe's, The Container Store, Southwest Airlines, Wegman's Food Markets, Commerce Bank, Best Buy, BMW, CarMax, eBay and more. Lo and behold, over a period of ten years, these firms of endearment wildly outperformed the rest of the corporate universe and continue to do so. We updated the FOE data to reflect the fifteen years between 1996 and 2011. On average, in that span, during which the benchmark S&P average was up 157 percent, FOE companies grew 1,646 percent. Over the last three economically fraught years, on an annualized basis, the S&P rose 3.3 percent. The FOE index was up 21.06 percent. Even allowing for the cherry-picking inherent in their choice of companies to study, Sisodia, Wolfe and Sheth demonstrated what Conrad Birdie sang fifty years ago: "You gotta be sincere."

So, then, how exactly does a business find itself in the happy circumstance of prospering by virtue of its cool and/or pretty self? We've already alluded to a few obvious things, all in the category of proscription, such as don't drop guitars on the tarmac. The proactive path, however, begins with nothing less human than introspection.

As an individual, you probably think about your purpose—the reason you get out of bed in the morning. We all want to provide value to the world, so why should we expect less of our organizations? Why are you in business? Why do you sell what you sell? Why do you drag your sorry butt out of bed at six o'clock in the morning? Here's a conversation that has never taken place:

"Honey, don't you want hit the snooze button?"
"Nah. I have to go maximize shareholder value."

First of all, short-term thinking aimed at propping up the stock price tends to lead to poor decisions, decisions that come back to haunt CEOs on their way to becoming former CEOs. What serves investors in the end is a strategy toward sustainable growth and return on equity. Rapid expansion, heedless acquisition, excessive cost-cutting, promotion-"purchased" market share and overextended debt can all pump up a stock, till one day comes the reckoning. What is immutable—and priceless—is a company or brand guided by the answer to "Why?" This exercise not only focuses the organization from top to bottom, it announces with every interaction with every stakeholder *what you are about* every hour of every day wherever you conduct your business—from the boardroom to the call center to the loading dock.

Brand Strategy

CONSUMER ERA	RELATIONSHIP ERA
Objective: Persuade consumers the brand has certain desirable attributes and benefits	**Objective:** Engage people on the brand's purpose
Strategy: Find and claim "white space" in consumers' minds	**Strategy:** Be clear about the brand's purpose and vision
Starts with: Consumer research	**Starts with:** Brand purpose discovery
Leads to: Campaign(s) to demonstrate positioning	**Leads to:** Movements that inspire people to join the brand
Creates: Brand positioning, which may change	**Creates:** Brand Stand, which is not likely to change
Success measure: Brand is associated with the new position	**Success measure:** Brand is known for its authentic stand

Happiness in a Carton

To derive brand purpose, corporate and brand stewards must understand what motivates them, what inspires them, what role they see for themselves and what role they see for the goods they put out in the world.

At Seventh Generation, the privately held organic cleaning products company, CEO John Replogle says, it's all about making a promise to posterity. "The essence of what we do is rooted in the great law of the Iroquois Indian and the great law says that in every deliberation, we will consider the impact of our decisions on the next seven generations. The whole relationship that we have with our consumers is founded on a couple of core principles about taking care of human health and environmental health and for being transparent and for having high integrity." This is because the corporate conscience demands it, and because increasingly the public demands it.

"More and more consumers today are shopping not simply from a front label," Replogle says. "They're flipping it over, checking out the back label to see what's in it. They are going even further to research the company that stands behind the brand and see if they affiliate with the essence and values of that company, and that's the good news about Seventh Generation."

For purity of purpose, it might be hard to top the spiritual link between man and earth. Articulating purpose, however, need not be spiritual nor even especially profound. The defining example is IKEA, which understood purpose before anybody thought to call it that. Founder Ingvar Kamprad had a set of founding values—honesty, inspiration, surprise, simplicity and affordability—distilled into a single commitment: "To create a better everyday life for the many." Decades later, the company has been unwavering, and its core commitment is manifest in every $2.99 *Snär* placemat, every $19.99 *Kvart* reading lamp and every $399 *Ektorp* sofa. High purpose is nice, but there is more than one way to skin a *katt*. There is no shame in the pragmatic, the practical, the market savvy, the enterprising . . . or even the accidental. Ask Tony Hsieh.

When he cofounded the shoes-by-mail sensation Zappos, Hsieh knew he could reduce prices by eliminating middlemen, duplicative warehousing and sales forces. And he believed that a simple, free, no-questions-asked return policy would compensate for the consumer habit of wanting to handle and try on the goods at retail. What he didn't know was that, despite phenomenal sales growth in the first two years, the only cash available to grow the business was his own. A series of national crises had dried up capital markets.

"There was 9/11, the war, recession, the dot-com bust," he says, "and so, we basically were forced to cut back our marketing—which ended being a blessing in disguise. That was how we ended up focusing on repeat customers and growing through word of mouth, because we didn't really have any other choice. Eventually that just became our business strategy. We just took most of the money we would have normally spent on paid advertising and paid marketing and decided to invest it into customer service and customer experience. So things like surprise upgrades to overnight shipping, running our call center 24/7, running our warehouse 24/7, all of that stuff is pretty expensive, but we really view those more as marketing dollars more than whatever they are normally categorized as."

And so, what started as circumstantial evolved into philosophical, and the business dedicated itself to "delivering happiness," a purpose that guides Zappos to this day. Customer experience with Zappos was so courteous, unscripted and accommodating—compared to the indifferent, flowcharted and unempowered call-center automatons we've all come to expect—that word of mouth exploded online. Maybe, strictly speaking, Zappos didn't deliver "happiness" (*delight* is probably a better word), but the company did deliver on its promises, and then some. "For example, as Hsieh says, it" upgrades its free surface shipping to surprise overnight delivery, also free to the customer. And giving customer reps unparalleled autonomy has created customer goodwill on practically a mythic scale. One Zappos employee stayed on a call for five hours to re-solve a customer issue. Hsieh tells a story about a Skechers sales rep in search of an after-hours meal. Hsieh swears he bet the salesman that a call to the Zappos 800 line would get him hooked up with dinner. Sure enough, the Zappos employee took the information and returned the call within five minutes with a list of pizzerias open near the guy's hotel.

With tales of positive experiences zipping every which way around the Internet, in spite of essentially zero advertising, Zappos sales grew from $1.6 million in 2000 to $184 million in 2004.[4] At that point, Sequoia Capital ponied up for a $35 million stake,[5] but the Zappos way had been established. The goofy corporate atmosphere, extremely liberal workplace policies and general celebration of quirky personalities were codified and incorporated into business practices across the board. Managers were encouraged to take subordinates out of the office during work hours to recreate. Cubicles were declared to be personal space to be dressed up as extravagantly or weirdly as the employee saw fit. Upon finishing training, new employees were offered $2,000 to quit—an early test of their dedication to the Zap-pos way.[6] A high premium was placed on personnel with personality and a genuine desire to help.

"We formalized the definition of our culture into ten core val-ues," Hsieh says. "I think when we started hiring for values, doing performance reviews in part based on values, that really forced us to focus on the fundamental idea being that we wanted people whose personal values matched the corporate values. That I think was when we started focusing a lot more on specifically who we are."

Eventually what they all became was a lot richer. In 2009, Ama-zon bought the company for $1.2 billion in cash and stock.[7]

If You Don't Believe Us, Ask Chuck

At precisely the same time Tony Hsieh was blundering on to his com-pany's reason for existing, another familiar company—also buffeted by 9/11 and the dot-com bust—was rediscovering its own. This would be Charles Schwab & Co., the pioneering discount brokerage turned full-service brokerage.

Schwab was founded in 1973 based on the idea of convenience, which manifested itself in market trades done by phone. In 1975, though, the SEC changed the rules allowing brokerage commissions to float, as opposed to the fixed rates long imposed by regulators. The white-shoe brokerage houses used the opportunity to raise commissions. Fledgling Charles Schwab & Co. lowered its own. That simple move spawned an industry dedicated to the most basic interests of the client: cost and convenience. Unsurprisingly, Schwab grew quickly and profitably. Throughout the 1990s, its stock outperformed Microsoft and Intel. In 1999, its market capitalization exceeded that of Merrill Lynch. In the year 2000, it was *Forbes* magazine's company of the year.[8]

Like many growing companies, Schwab expanded its scope and its offerings. In 2000, it spent just shy of $3 billion to acquire the bank holding company U.S. Trust.[9] It invested in an equities-research subsidiary. It expanded globally and built out its institutional brokerage capacities. Then came those back-to-back calamities of 9/11 and the dot-com bust. At that point, according to long-standing transition plans, Charles Schwab himself stepped aside from his co-CEO duties. But eighteen months later, during a 26 percent decline in brokerage revenue and a stock that had plummeted from a historical high of $50 to $9 a share, the board brought him back. The founder found a bloated, stagnant, overextended company that had lost touch with its founding principles. The company's Net Promoter Score, probably the most widely adopted metric of customer-relations management on the globe, languished at −34.[10] "We need," Schwab concluded, "to reconnect with our clients." So he did what corporate Mr. Fixits do, even ones who started the companies they need to fix. He cut senior management. He laid off workers. He shed extraneous businesses. He lowered the fixed brokerage commission his predecessor had raised, and he set out to repair what had become woeful customer service.

Shortly thereafter, management promulgated a list of twelve Guiding Principles. Here are a few that caught our attention:

1. Every client interaction changes our company's future—either to the positive or to the negative.
2. The majority of attainable revenue growth is a function of delighting our existing clients—which leads to increased business and referrals to new prospects.
3. Clients value relationships—with people and organizations that they have confidence in, trust will act in their best interest and help them reach their financial goals.
5. We improve the client experience by listening to clients at every opportunity—and acting on what we learn.
7. We will view each client as a whole person—offering a seamless client experience that reflects his or her total business at Schwab (brokerage, bank, 401k).
6. Investing in our people is core to our success today and in the future.[11]

Sound familiar? We acknowledge that the twelve Principles do not, strictly speaking, constitute a single core purpose. But we should also point out that when Schwab returned, the company's client assets had dipped to $942 billion. Today they sit at $1.8 trillion. That's a doubling. Brokerage accounts have grown from 7 million to 8.7 million. That's an increase of 24 percent. And the Net Promoter Score has risen 75 points to +41, which is Nordstrom territory.[12] So, yeah, as the ad slogan suggests, "Talk to Chuck." He seems to be listening.

Putting Your Money Where Your Mouth Is

The quest for corporate purpose, needless to say, isn't always so dramatic, and it needn't be as lofty as delivering happiness. This is not about ministry; it's simply about knowing your mind. There is plenty of room for less ambitious goals and less ambitious motivations, so long as they faithfully distill the brand's *raison d'être* and aren't simply profit driven. This hypothetical would do the trick, for instance: "To make an impact by manufacturing our product at such low cost that it will be affordable to virtually every living soul on the globe." That purpose wouldn't necessarily bring a tear to anyone's eye, and it clearly envisions massive revenue, but it also embodies at least as much sense of mission as it does strategy. That said, some of the more remarkable and inspiring case histories belong to companies whose definition of purpose so hinges on human values (apparently) antithetical to ordinary business practices that management must violate the principles of the Four Ps left, right and center. Here's how the outdoors outfitter Patagonia defines its reason for being: Build the best product, cause no unnecessary harm, use business to inspire and implement solutions to the environmental crisis.[13]

This has been the Patagonia way for forty years, since founder Yvon Chouinard set up shop to outfit lovers of the outdoors without contributing to the destruction of the outdoors. The company donates 1 percent of its gross sales to environmental causes,[14] recruits other businesses to do the same and engineers every aspect of its operation toward source reduction and environmental sustainability. It has progressive workplace polices—from in-house day care to paternity leave to paid sabbaticals for environmental volunteerism[15]— and enforces identical factory conditions whether in California or Vietnam.[16] It was years ahead of government regulators committing to reducing to zero, by 2015, toxic discharge anywhere in its supply chain. And, in 1996, it made a very expensive decision to use only organic cotton in its cotton goods.[17] CEO Casey Sheehan recalls the corporate thinking at the time: "For a period of years, our margins will suffer, our prices will be high, but we will also tell the world that we are doing this because if we don't do this and the world continues down the path of using conventional cotton, we are going to use up all the water and turn these agricultural areas into pesticide ridden areas."

None of this eco-righteousness has thus far ravaged the bottom line. On the contrary.

"The last three and a half years," Sheehan says, "have been the best years in Patagonia history—and that's from the revenue growth, operating income, all the traditional measurements. . . . We've expanded our annual profit from 2%–3% back in the day to now in the 9% range annually. That's right on par with public-company metrics."

Oh, and this transpired in the middle of the worst economy since the Dust Bowl. Patagonia's annual employee turnover is 5 percent. Their percentage of rejected goods at the factory is 1 percent.[18] So confident is Patagonia about its business, and its worldview, that it took full-page ads in major newspapers before Christmas in 2011 and implored its customers *not to be* customers. Reminiscent of the famous Volkswagen "lemon" exercise that commenced advertising's so-called Creative Revolution, the Patagonia ad displayed a handsome parka above a headline that admonished, "Don't buy this jacket," whereupon the text delineated the environmental toll of a single piece of Patagonia outerwear. The implicit message, though, was this: Don't buy our jacket unless you really need one, in which case, now that you understand our seriousness, why would you buy from anyone else?"[19] On lesser emotional and rational underpinnings entire cults have formed. It's not just Pollyanna happy talk. It's the marketing of principle, which is possible exactly to the extent that it is genuine.

"There is nothing Kumbaya about it," Sheehan feels obliged to point out. "It's just that everything you say and do and the energy you project has the potential to affect everyone around you. The people you work with, the people you contract with. It's simple: A happy CEO or leader means happy workers which means happy products, happy customers."

That is why Relationship Era thinking cannot be isolated to the C-suite. It must be internalized by all management and must inform every corporate relationship, from contract workers to securities analysts. In a recent *Harvard Business Review* article, then-visiting professor Modesto Maidique reimagined leadership by posing a seminal question to his top-level audience: "Whom do you serve? Yourself? Your group? Society? Wall Street?" We subsequently asked him what he was getting at. After all, isn't keeping the stock price up a CEO's primary fiduciary responsibility?

"People assess corporate success based on stockholder returns," says Maidique, director of the Center for Leadership at Florida International University. "You look at the most return and that's the best CEO." But in a hyperconnected world, he says, the boss must be a steward of the entire ecosystem. Information is everywhere, and "the approach they take to their ecosystem is going to be widely reported around the world." Whereas author and Nestlé executive Pete Blackshaw has famously asserted "Customer service is the new media department,"[20] if Maidique is right, *everything* you do is the new media department.

E *verything* you do is the new media department.

I Deep Fry, Therefore I Am

Perhaps you're thinking: "No kidding? Obviously, people in glass houses shouldn't lounge around in their underwear." Or perhaps: "Sure, some whole-grained, tree-hugging mother earthlings like Seventh Generation and Patagonia manage to build a business out of twigs and bark, but aren't they profiting from a preexisting global movement and have a customer base predisposed to buying in?" So let's consider a very different sort of enterprise, one that not only sells among the most nutritionally incorrect products on earth but for good measure has spent most of the millennium so far as a laughingstock on Wall Street.

We refer, of course, to Krispy Kreme Doughnuts. Having plummeted from $44 per share in 2003 to $1.15 in 2009—when overexpansion, accounting irregularities and investors' sudden loss of irrational exuberance finally ended what had been three-plus years of Krispy Kre-mania—its stock has climbed back to the $7 to $9 range on the strength of steadily growing revenue, profit, same-store sales and the nearly insane devotion of its fans everywhere.

"You look at our fans and no matter what happens, they love us," says CMO Dwayne Chambers. "People like to eat doughnuts when they are really happy and people like to eat doughnuts when they are maybe worried or they may be a little melancholy for the day. We have one of those products that really fits a lot of different needs and a lot of different emotions." Like a friend—a glazed or cream-filled friend.

The company's gradual resurgence began with the 2009 hiring of CEO Jim Morgan, who presided over management introspection about Krispy Kreme's corporate purpose. What came out of this process was nothing particularly sophisticated. If anything, it resembled old-time religion: "Touching and enhancing people's lives through the joy that is Krispy Kreme."[21] The executives didn't decree so; they distilled the watchword from seventy-five years in the guilty-pleasure industry. What they decreed was that the joy ethic inform every interaction at every level of the business—which is a bit like ordering a fish to swim. The idea of cultivating those human-to-human relationships ran deep in Krispy Kreme "kulture."

"The brand was always built on word of mouth, which was the social media of decades prior," Chambers says. "It was the man or woman going to the barber shop or beauty shop and chatting about a product or business. . . . But when you look at something like social media and the ability to engage people in conversation, and truly engage in their conversation about what they're interested in, all of a sudden now, you are at a much deeper level in your ability to do that."

So long as you remember the difference between staying connected and using social-media channels to send 140-character ads. Whereas KFC, for instance, uses Twitter to sell, sell, sell, Krispy Kreme uses it to engage, engage, engage.

@krispykreme Wasn't that a sweet moment? RT@drmarsch: Oscar Meyer Wiener Mobile and Krispy Kreme Cruiser meet by chance. pic.twitter.com/JyLmh9OT

Chambers: "If you think about if you are sitting at your house and in front of your computer and you are working along, and a friend of yours sends you an email, no matter what you're doing, you're going to stop what you are doing and click on that email because it's a friend of yours and you want to know what's going on, because they wouldn't send you an email unless there's a reason. We want to be in that category."

A tall order. But when there is congruency between the expressed and observable values of the brand and those of the brand's constituencies, an actual sense of belonging sets in and remarkable dynamics commence. Not only do the folks at Krispy Kreme find it easier to bounce out of bed not at six but at four o'clock in the morning to fire up the ovens, they require less and less expensive advertising to sell more and more hot and delicious cardiovascular time bombs. Paid media, says Chambers, represents less than 5 percent of his budget. With 3.8 million Facebook followers, he doesn't need big media budgets to engage with humanity.

Love Is Blue (Cheese)

In the early afternoon one day last spring in Naples, Florida, Bostonian Fred Reichheld took his son Jimmy into a quick-serve joint for lunch. They'd just finished eighteen holes of golf at Tiburon and needed to fill the tank. The place was a chain restaurant with very little presence where they live, so this promised to be an exotic experience. Jimmy had never been in a Chick-fil-A.

"Very clean, nice restaurant," recalls Fred, "but then this friendly lady walks up to us and wants to know if she can refill our drinks. Which is one of their things they do to wow customers. We really didn't want our drinks refilled, but she was chatty and she said, 'Oh, you're eating that spicy chicken sandwich. I love that! Have you ever tried that with blue cheese dressing like you use on buffalo wings?' I said, 'No, I've never tried that.' She said, 'Do you like blue cheese dressing?' I said, 'Yeah, sometimes.' So she runs back into the kitchen and gets a packet of dressing that they use for their salads and said, 'Here, try this on it.' And I did and it was wonderful and in the process she started kidding around with my son. She said, 'Listen, we've got family night tonight and the kids all get to decorate cupcakes and then they get free chicken nuggets!'"

Which was adorable, because Jimmy was twenty-two.

"He thought that was cute, and then she described all the things they do in the store to make it a really delightful experience, whether it's a family night, or a daddy-daughter date night." For that, she explained to the guests, there is lace to adorn the tables, the staff wears formal clothing and the store hires a horse and carriage to deliver the couples from the parking lot to the door. Then she told them about the store's solution for soccer moms and other hapless adults trying to feed a van full of amped-up little demons.

Her explanation, as he tells it: "'It's sort of hectic and they are trying to keep their kids under control, so what we've encouraged them to do is go to the drive-in window and place their order while the kids are still in the seat belts. So they will drive through, and park and then come [inside] and we bring the food to them and it's all organized and ready to go.'"

All of the above being simply music to Fred Reichheld's ears, because Chick-fil-A happens to be a client of his, and he happens to be the inventor of the aforementioned Net Promoter Score. This cheerful employee had no idea, but she was sharing all this enthusiasm with the living soul most associated with employee enthusiasm as a bankable asset. But because to her he was just a hungry guy in golf togs, the episode was pure. It was *fil-A* of kindness. It was one human being just connecting in a human way with two other humans.

Fred Reichheld was experiencing in person what up to that point had been just an extremely gaudy statistic: the highest Net Promoter Score in the fast-food business. Chick-fil-A's deeply ingrained hospitality, though, is a direct result of a business operating with an absolutely religious sense of purpose. And we don't mean "religious" metaphorically. The company's mission, as printed on the back of every Chick-fil-A business card: "To glorify God by being a faithful steward of all that is entrusted to us. To have a positive influence on all who come in contact with Chick-fil-A."[22]

We are not proselytizing on behalf of corporate religiosity; on the contrary, we take deep exception to the company's activism against gay marriage, a stance that in July 2012 provoked a boycott (and two months later a reversal of corporate policy) after the company's president released a statement verifying political contributions to anti-gay organizations. But we must observe that by cleaving faithfully to its particular purpose, Chick-fil-A exudes its Chick-fil-A-ness across the board. And, as with Krispy Kreme and Zappos, the rewards are not merely spiritual. On a per-dollar-of-revenue basis, Chick-fil-A spends one-third of what McDonald's does on advertising. To be precise: McDonald's spends 2.6 percent of gross revenue. Chick-Fil-A spends .84 percent. The rest flows to the bottom line—because, says Reichheld, "You don't need that level of advertising if your customers are walking advertisements for you."

While You're Out, Grab Me a Skinny Latte Grande and a Reputation

Impressive, no? That's the kind of eye-popping cost savings that prompts some CEOs to look deep into their own souls for a corporate *raison d'être*, and many others to summon the p.r. people into the C-suite to puff up their image. This process tends to end with some fatuous social-media stunts and a rewritten corporate mission statement—which is to say, fools' errands.

All social efforts must flow from an authentic sense of purpose, not gimmickry and transparently bogus boilerplate. Otherwise, says Jeremy Heimans of the Purpose agency, "you've become McDonald's, where you end up prematurely declaring victory because you've implemented a salad on your menu."

Core values cannot be faked—or, anyway, not indefinitely. Scott Adams, of Dilbert fame, once created a mission statement generator, which could be loaded with a few familiar buzzwords to automatically formulate high-toned bullshit ("Our challenge is to assertively network economically sound methods of empowerment so that we may continually negotiate performance-based infrastructures").

Pretty funny. But if you really want a hearty laugh, check out the actual "values statement" for Philip Morris. Item No. 1, as God is our witness: "Integrity, trust and respect."[23] Here's another, literally etched in stone in the lobby of a corporate headquarters: "Integrity. Communication. Respect. Excellence." The corporation? Why, Enron, of course.[24] The message would have been longer, but the stonemason ran out of room to chisel in "Rapacious Jackals."

Hyping dubious humanity credentials is like lying to your psychoanalyst; it's a pointless exercise. Furthermore, do not confuse genuine purpose with other notions of differentiation, such as "positioning" rooted in a manipulation or contrivance. Empty mottos and positioning are just posturing, expressions of "what can we *say* about our brand that sets us apart." Marketing from purpose is no less differentiating, but sets a brand apart from its demonstrated character. It can be banal "to perfect and share the most delicious ice cream" or it can be lofty, but it must explain to all comers why you are in business.

Hyping dubious humanity credentials is like lying to your psychoanalyst; it's a pointless exercise.

Oh, and also be, you know . . . true.

Even the most publicized brand-sponsored, crowd-sourced do-gooderism of the recent past—the Pepsi Refresh Project—failed to pass the authenticity test. Yes, the brand gave away $20 million to applicants seeking to effect positive change in their own communities. Yes, it gleaned priceless publicity in hundreds of locales. And, yes, it built the project around the choices of a new generation: the pet causes of the idealistic young people it has long cultivated through advertising. But it was not matched by significant efforts within PepsiCo to ameliorate its own impact on, say, community health.

"When we do our work," says Jeremy Heimans, "one of our criteria is what is the net impact of this company on the world must be positive. If it's not positive, then the question is 'Can we enable serious internal transformation, and not just do something that's really good, but just marginal or peripheral?' Pepsi Refresh was a marketing campaign that basically had nothing to do with changing PepsiCo's economic engine. Their core economic engine is sugar and salt, which is very bad for the world."

If that sounds harsh, listen to the conclusions of the Berkeley Media Studies Group, which dismissed Pepsi Refresh as a thinly veiled corporate social responsibility effort to change the subject from the linkage between sugary drinks and the obesity epidemic. "Innocence by association," the academics called it, and then the criticism got worse, because Pepsi Refresh reminded them of something: "These campaigns echo the tobacco industry's use of CSR as a means to focus responsibility on consumers rather than on the corporation, bolster the companies' and their products' popularity, and to prevent regulation."[25]

The *tobacco* industry? Ouch.

All of which is to say, operating from purpose is really quite simple . . . except for being very, very hard. It's hard because such thinking goes against the grain, the instincts, the experience and the formal education of most everybody in the business world. They have consumer demand imprinted in their minds and TV ROI models open on their desktops. Anyone evangelizing about leading the consumer, versus catering to the consumer, is dismissed as an apostate, an ignoramus or maybe just a total crackpot. Eric Ryan, a refugee from the Consumer Era, remembers his frustration as an ad-agency planner trying to get people even to consider his thoughts on a brand's self-determined point of view.

"It's impossible to lead the consumer because you are always just following them," he recalls of the bad old days. "I used to get my hands slapped in the advertising world, because as a planner, you are supposed to be the voice of the consumer but I always loved mingling the voice of the consumer with what I thought would be a unique perspective or point of view for a brand.

"When I was at Hal Riney [& Partners advertising on the Saturn car account], I began spending more time with the car studios and the tech center, helping the designers of the cars. I remember being pulled aside and told 'We don't make money by helping them build better cars. We make money by making better ads.'"

Ad Agencies Against Purpose

Flash forward and now the agency guy is the client. Ryan is CEO of Method, the organic home products company organized around a core purpose that also happens to be its slogan: "People against dirty."[26]

He and his cofounder, Adam Lowry, know exactly what they are about. Their soaps and detergents are made with plant-based compounds and natural fragrances, not caustic chemicals, and are packaged in stylish, 100 percent post-consumer-recycled containers verging on *objets d'art*. Method products are designed to be their own advertisements, to exude the brand's personality, to capture the imagination of the shopper traipsing down Target's aisles. Should the shopper be curious enough to see what the teardrop-shaped bottle is all about, or the *pump* of laundry detergent, she might see a message embossed underneath: "Stop looking at my bottom." Yes, there's a bit of madness to the Method, but absolutely method to the madness. "We are just trying to catch people in all of these little human ways," Ryan says. "We didn't want a campaign; we wanted a movement."

And yet, now that he is the client for the ad agencies working with Method, Ryan still faces the same stubborn resistance to a brand standing for what the brand simply is. Based on what they believe will most resonate in the marketplace, he says, "agencies usually go in and want to start reworking the brand and what the brand is and what the brand stands for. . . . Usually the first thing I get back is a deck saying why 'People against dirty' is not a good way to move forward. . . . It's always been a battle."

Not just with his agencies, but with the retail trade.

"I always get asked 'When are you guys going to do more advertising?' Retailers are so trained on how much money you spend. Retailers want scale, scale, scale."

Still, he and Lowry press on . . . because they can. There is no Wall Street pressuring them to use artificial fragrances at half the cost of natural ones, or virgin plastic instead of more pricey 100 percent recycled. Yet twelve years into its history Method is among the fastest-growing private companies in America. As ex-Dell CMO Erin Nelson lectured the Association of National Advertisers not long ago, "Purpose isn't just good for the soul, it's actually really good for the bottom line."[27]

Lumbering Along

Such is the fondest hope of Kyle Schlegel, CMO of Hillerich & Bradsby, makers of the Louisville Slugger. When he arrived at the company in February 2012, fresh out of senior brand management in the hair-care category at Procter & Gamble, he found a venerable, 129-year-old family business barely caught up to the Consumer Era, much less the brave new world.

"We were starting from scratch," he says, "and I think that made it easier to build purpose into the way we go about marketing the brand because there were not a lot of sacred cows that you had to battle with."

Right, purpose. At Procter he had been through the purpose process for two brands, an experience he found to be endlessly rewarding and endlessly frustrating. Rewarding for all the reasons stated above, and frustrating because—despite all the glowing rhetoric and stated C-suite support—when push came to shove, the actual P&G brand management system was constructed on very different values. Careers are propelled by moving the needle right now. Some brands (Secret antiperspirant, as you shall soon learn, among them) enthusiastically embraced purpose, but others did not because there was meager penalty for lack of enthusiasm.

"Many of them almost feel like they are choosing," Schlegel says, "between a purpose-inspired activity versus a tactical, down-and-dirty, 'I need to stack it high and sell it low at Wal-Mart.' And so that connection is elusive for a lot of people.

"How to make purpose tangible is something that I think I still struggle with to some degree today. As with any team, there were folks who were more comfortable in that broad kind of dreaming space and there were those who were more comfortable in the numerics and what's on the spreadsheet."

Resolving those conflicts is the most difficult aspect of navigating the paradigm shift into Relationship Era marketing. Yet, at H&B, Schlegel was singularly advantaged. He had been hired by a CEO, Bill Clark, who had long since determined that Louisville Slugger would operate out of core beliefs, not bottom-line venality—a determination that ran deep in the brand's heritage.

"We are the only family-owned, privately held brand really left in the space. Everybody else has been bought up by equity firms or larger sporting goods companies. They have very deep pockets and a lot of influence. Really our influence comes back to our brand name."

The bad news is that those deep-pocketed competitors are at the moment cleaning H&B's clock. The good news is that Schlegel's expedition into the soul of the company yielded assets no competitor can match. The Louisville Slugger has not just a noble history but holds a mythic place in the national psyche. The Slugger's first professional endorser was Honus Wagner.

"This brand and this brand alone is the one that can reignite that emotional connection to the game of baseball that's been lost a little bit in today's instant-gratification culture," Schlegel says. "Baseball is not an easy sport to sit and watch for three hours, whereas football and basketball and others are easier to do so. But there is something so American in that, so father-handing-down-to-son. We knew that was very important in re-creating or reigniting that emotional connection to the brand."

The question was: 'Is that emotion simply the function of longevity, or does the Louisville Slugger legacy owe itself to something intrinsic about the brand? Have they just sold bats since the Chester Arthur administration, or is there something deeper there to be plumbed and developed?'

"We went back to, 'What is that intersection between us and our consumer?' You get back to Venn diagrams and all that. You come back to what is that intersection between what it is that we are about and what we can offer, not in just the shampoo aisle, or the sporting goods aisle, but 'What is it that we can offer to this industry, to humanity, and then how does that interact with the basic needs, wants, desires of the people that you are seeking to talk with?'"

Working through MEplusYOU's purpose-discovery process, the newly formed executive team, at very great length, was able to distill what the company cares about to a clear set of beliefs:

> We believe that lasting greatness is only achieved by living the values of team sports, driven by sportsmanship, hard work and dedication.
>
> We believe that confidence is the most valuable tool you bring toward your game.
>
> We believe that working with elite athletes leads to the creation of elite products.
>
> We believe we have the responsibility to grow and protect the Louisville Slugger as an American icon.

These beliefs were the foundation for a single brand purpose: *We exist to make players great.*

So far, so good. Alas, no less than at Procter & Gamble, such deep understanding does not necessarily all at once create windfalls. Ball bats are purchased for children, who drive the brand decisions, and for the most part neither Slugger's purpose nor its rich legacy means squat to them. Other brands, such as Easton, Nike, Marucci and DeMarini, have established reputations for high performance and captured the imaginations of a generation that doesn't really care what bat Honus Wagner used. The kids were all too well aware of the quality gap. Complicating problems, some competitors offered higher performance by exceeding limits of elasticity (called the batted ball coefficient of restitution) imposed for safety of fielders. Two models of Marucci bats, for instance, have been ruled by the NCAA and youth baseball organizations as noncompliant.[28]

Without naming names, Schlegel asserts that various competitors not only flout those safety standards but use Louisville Slugger-contracted Major League Baseball players in advertising and undersell their own retailers in direct sales. Under such circumstances, he says, the company thinks about its values very, very hard.

"We certainly believe that they are not living by that same code and that's frustrating sometimes. You see a competitor acting in a way that is frankly benefiting them, and your first reaction is, 'Well if they are doing it, we should do it too.' But we've continued to come back to, 'No, that's actually not the way that we are going to operate. We believe in this point of *lasting* greatness.

"We've been around 128 years because we've done things the right way. The marketplace knows we are nice, good guys. We are going to do things with their best interest in mind and we are going to continue to come back to that."

Nice guys, he is convinced, will finish first. With the introduction of several higher-performance products and a new focus on its brand values, in the first fiscal year following the retooling of the brand, Slugger was on a trajectory for 10 to 15 percent sales growth. In the meantime, not only does Schlegel bounce out of bed in the morning, he sleeps well at night.

"I think we all go through this process, right? I mean, I remember getting out of college and thinking, 'Why am I here? What am I here for?' You go through that soul searching."

He can't prove the business will explode, but Schlegel has found what he was looking for.

The Wrong Path

Finding what you're looking for. One wonders: Can Rupert Murdoch make that claim?

Murdoch, of course, built News Corp., one of the world's largest media empires, by ruthlessly serving growth and profitability. It was not merely a strategy; it was a credo, as articulated by his son and then presumed successor James in 2009 at the MediaGuardian Edinburgh International Television Festival. Profit, said James Murdoch, is "the only reliable, durable, and perpetual guarantor of independence."

Within two years of uttering that statement, James Murdoch's News Group Newspapers subsidiary and the whole of News Corp. was in disarray. A 2011 scandal related to voice mail hacking by the *News of the World* tabloid unraveled into shocking revelations about cover-up, bribery and influence peddling at the highest levels of British government. By early 2012 there had been more than sixty arrests and the shuttering of *News of the World*. The younger Murdoch was forced to resign first as chairman of News Group Newspapers and then as executive chairman of News Corp.'s newspaper arm. And before the summer was out, News Corp. was preparing to spin off its newspaper properties lest they drag down the rest of the empire.

That was the situation in August 2012, when James's sister Elisabeth, chairman of News Corp.'s Shine TV production subsidiary, herself delivered the James MacTaggart Memorial keynote at the conference. She did not espouse the family values. On the contrary, she repudiated the parent company's philosophy in stark terms. Whereas James had claimed that single-minded focus on profit yielded editorial independence, which in turn guaranteed a free press and democracy itself, Elisabeth concluded that "sadly the greatest threats to our free society are too often from enemies within. . . . One of the biggest lessons of the past year has been the need for any organization to discuss, affirm and institutionalize a rigorous set of values based on an explicit statement of purpose.

"Profit without purpose," she said, "is a recipe for disaster."

5

SUSTAIN

Every profession bears the responsibility to understand the
circumstances that enable its existence.

—ROBERT GUTMAN, ARCHITECT

Plant azaleas.

Begonias, petunias and impatiens are lovely, but every year you have to start over with them. That means buying them and planting them and watering them, only to see them wither and die in the fall. Azaleas are perennial. Take reasonable care with them and they will flower beautifully year after year.

See where this is going? Ad campaigns are trays of bedding plants. The Relationship Era is a garden full of azaleas. As we have seen in examples of Chick-fil-A and Krispy Kreme, the most visible advantage of brand sustainability is the azalea effect—the diminished need to buy large quantities of advertising. Though we haven't collected brand sustainability data on Panera Bread, CEO Ron Shaich says his ad spending is 1 percent of sales. The casual-dining category as a whole spends 3 to 5 percent. The Zappos ad budget is near zero. Here's another look at the Brand Sustainability Map, this time focusing on the retail category:

BRAND SUSTAINABILITY MAP

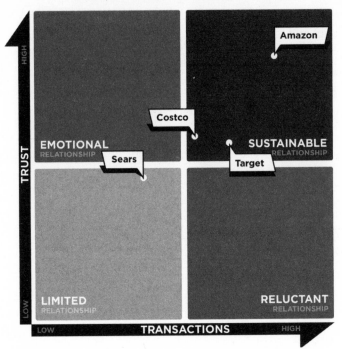

Note that three retailers in the "sustainable" quadrant—Amazon, Costco and Target—spend on average .52 percent of sales on measured media. Sears, buried in the "limited" quadrant, spends 1.62 percent of sales—and loses market share doing it. It's not difficult to see why organizing brands around positive ongoing relationships versus gross ratings points makes a lot of sense. But not to everybody, apparently. Remember the Google experiment that began Chapter 2? Searching for "I love _____" to see what turned up? Two of the most dismal results were scored by two historically massive advertising spenders, Citibank and AT&T Wireless. One of them has decided, belatedly, to plant azaleas.

Not a big surprise. It's not hard to rethink things when you've been saved from total oblivion thanks only to the $100 billion largesse of the U.S. government. Now, you can blame Citi's near collapse on the 1999 repeal of the Glass-Steagall Act, as ex-CEO

Richard Parsons did upon his April 2012 retirement. And you'd be right. Or you can blame it on the utter incompetence of ratings agencies and federal regulators that failed to see the financial industry's insane overexposure to risk a decade ago. And you'd be right. Or you can blame the greed and fraud on Wall Street in the haphazard securitizing of mortgage debt and the physics-defying leverage it camouflaged with credit default swaps. And you'd be right. Or you could blame the greed and delusional behavior of Joe Mortgage Applicant, who signed onto debt burdens he couldn't reasonably expect to shoulder. And you'd be right. Or you could blame the greed and fiduciary irresponsibility among Citi and other banks for both originating dubious subprime loans and off-loading the hidden risks in a feeding frenzy of fees they gorged upon on all sides of the transactions, right up until the bubble burst on the entire world.

But here's the thing: Lehman Brothers is dead and Moody's, the rating agency, doesn't send you a credit card bill every month or hammer you with checking fees. Citi, on the other hand, is on every street corner and has been on TV for decades, promising you how trustworthy it is. The bank is therefore very handy if you're looking for a scapegoat. So, yeah, as a brand, it had some work to do.

"Citi did not waste this crisis," says Vanessa Colella, managing director and head of North America marketing at Citibank. "There was a tremendous amount of introspection."

Also a tremendous amount of turnover, including the additions of Citigroup CEO Vikram Pandit, North America consumer bank CEO Manuel Medina-Mora and Colella herself.

"We've got a whole new set of executives in the consumer bank here and I think we all came in with the attitude of we have a lot of fixing to do here," she says. "I personally came to Citi because I believed that the country deserves Citi to be better. And the 110,000 people that we employ in the U.S. . . . deserve to be proud of where they work. And we had failed. So it was all about how do you start from that point on that journey and do right by people?"

Suffice it to say Colella is under no illusions about the difficulties of such a "journey." Odysseus had it easier, and he faced sirens, giant cannibals, Cyclops and Circe, who turned men into pigs but never foreclosed on anybody.

"I think the consumer mistrust is ours to fix but obviously not under our control," Colella says. "In fact, when I first got here, I used to liken it to a soured relationship. You can't have a relationship go bad and then just show up one day with a ring and expect to get married. It's a long process of re-wooing, if you will, and demonstrating continued value. There are a lot of initiatives at Citi to demonstrate that value to consumers, but it's a journey and we certainly feel like we are just at the beginning."

The beginning of the beginning (corresponding neatly to the advice we shall presently issue) was a large-scale listening offensive. This included Net Promoter Score surveys, live and online focus groups, feedback from consumer touch points such as phone, e-mail, chat and, of course, social media.

"We spent probably the first eighteen months in social listening. At this point we've got hundreds of customer service reps trained on Twitter . . . to respond to customer inquiries . . . We interrupt over a thousand conversations a week, be it on Twitter, Facebook, but also on a lot of the popular blogs."

They interrupt not by tweeting "Shut up," but by asking the dissatisfied customer for details and trying to ameliorate the complaint as it surfaces. The exercise was illuminating, if not necessarily heartening. In the entire financial services industry, it appeared, "Citi was at the bottom of the barrel, not that it's such a glorious industry to begin with."

The very direness of the situation, though, emboldened the C-suite. They knew their odyssey, however difficult and frightening, must continue. And slowly they began implementing measures to rebuild the consumer bank around the, you know, consumers. One quick fix was to allow call-center reps on the banking side of the business to resolve the ten most frequently asked questions from credit card customers mistakenly dialing the bank, thus preventing innumerable unnecessary call transfers into the purgatory of the credit side's hold queue—where the Muzak does nothing to diminish consumer frustration. Another simple matter was to build click-to-call functionality into social responses; you complain or raise a question on Twitter and Citi tweets back, giving you a one-click link to customer service. Then there was training of frontline employees, such as tellers and call-center personnel, who for the first time were given access to the customer's entire portfolio of Citi business, allowing them to take a 360-degree approach in any inter-action. Then there were simple atmospherics. If you called the bank to modify your mortgage, instead of being connected to a "loss mit-igation specialist," you'd speak to a "homeowner support specialist." Colella insists this shift signified far more than simple semantics. "This is more than a name change," she says. "It's meant to reinforce our customer-first culture. We have also moved to a single-point-of-contact approach for homeowners in need."

Indeed, addressing people in need has been the center of Citi's attempt to redefine itself, and CitiMortgage was pretty much ground zero. It began in November 2008 with the Citi Homeowner Assis-tance Program (CHAP), designed to be a kind of first responder for those in present, imminent or a potential mortgage crisis. Responses ranged from sharing FAQ (and the answers) to temporary mortgage payment reductions for the unemployed to foreclosure moratoriums at Christmas and in the aftermath of the Gulf of Mexico oil spill. In April 2011, the bank initiated a project dubbed Road to Recovery, deploying homeowner support specialists to the twenty-five U.S. cit-ies hardest hit by the real estate crash. This effort attracted twenty-three hundred mortgage holders, of which two-thirds were able to come to, in Colella's words, "some type of a solution." Then, "in De-cember 2011, we launched HomeownerSupport.com, an online com-munity where anyone can learn about various options for mortgage support and where—through forums and outreach from a Citi com-munity manager—customers can engage in timely dialogue, often with each other. In addition to this site, we also actively engage in listening and conversations across the Web where we believe we might be able to offer information or a solution. Listening has helped us change more than processes. It also has driven very real, very hu-man benefits that are easily seen in changes within our CitiMortgage business."

Of all the new approaches and processes, Colella believes the "biggest leap forward" is transparency, with regulators, shareholders and customers alike, which she characterizes as "quite distinct from some of our competitors." More subtle is the trade-off between the long journey of changing the culture and the short-term responsibilities to Wall Street.

"We are all business people. There is a clear understanding that we have to find a way to do that while we are flying the plane. We've got shareholder and analyst expectations that we need to meet and we try to make the best decisions that will deliver financial results and that will get us to the right long-term place. You just have to be a prudent manager about what you are investing in and be really careful about measuring when it's going to pay off. To me, that's just our job."

Wall Street was not particularly quick to embrace the new path; Citigroup's share price, which had neared $700 before the crash, has languished in the $20 to $42 range since early 2009. CEO Pandit suddenly "resigned" in October 2012, though by mid-2011 earnings had begun to pick up, and the long-suspended dividend was restored. At least as importantly for Colella, the customer-satisfaction metrics reflect dramatic improvement. Citi's credit card division scores on Forrester's 2011 Customer Experience Index rose from 50 in 2010 to 62 in 2011, which while still pretty horrendous on a 100-point scale is nonetheless a 24 percent improvement in one year.[1] At a time when the public hates banks more than it hates bank robbers, that's on the verge of astonishing.

"We're here to reshape this company around our customers and that is a long term goal," she says. "And that's what motivates us and gets us up in the morning and makes us want to do better tomorrow than we did today."

So that's the azalea approach. For the tray-of-petunias status quo, the place to look is AT&T Wireless. At the 2012 Ad Age Digital Conference, AT&T's VP for brand identity and design Gregg Heard wondered aloud why the company that delivers smartphone magic isn't more beloved. The very idea, according to *Ad Age*'s ensuing article, was met by the audience with skepticism. "You could hear crickets," reported Kunur Patel, "and a few giggles."[2]

"What we want you to think," Heard continued, according to *Ad Age*, "is that AT&T is an emotional lifestyle brand that lets you live your life more expansively and brings you new experiences and new value. But that's just not the perception. . . . All major carriers are facing [the] same perception challenge: People really love their technology but don't love their carrier."[3]

The key words in that passage are "what we want you to think." In the Relationship Era, not to put too fine a point on it, nobody cares what the brand wants us to think. We think what we think, which is largely a reflection of what those we trust think, and one entity whose customers do not trust it at all is AT&T Wireless. The brand's solution for dealing with the supposed perception gap is therefore retrograde and futile: changing the "Rethink Possible" advertising campaign. "We're shifting to focus on how technology is enabling our life," Heard told his colleagues.[4] That means instead of announcing to an increasingly small and inattentive audience that AT&T offers the best coverage and connection speed, the brand will announce to an increasingly small and inattentive audience that the brand is part of users' most significant moments in life. Cue the commercial showing the actress playing an actress telling her friends she just snagged a big part.

Yes, a telecom brand incapable of, ahem, connecting with its customers addresses the problem by *changing its positioning*. Someone there needs to rethink impossible.

A Word on Methodology

AT&T's place on the Brand Sustainability Map clearly illustrates its place in the consumer imagination.

The goal of the BSM was to show the relationship between contemporaneous market success and the qualities associated with future success. Thus the lower right "reluctant" quadrant would contain dominant brands with dubious long-term prospects, the upper left "emotional" quadrant would contain trusted brands with competitive disadvantages (such as price or distribution) but the prerequisites

BRAND SUSTAINABILITY MAP

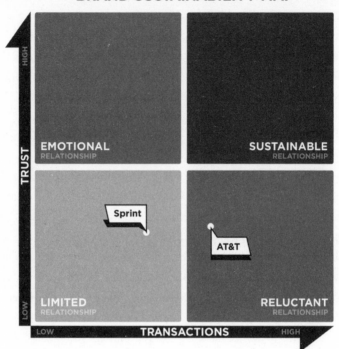

for long-term success, and "sustainable" brands would be dominant now and in the foreseeable future. The lower left "limited" quadrant would mean trouble. Trouble now and trouble later.

The problem dictated the solution: a graph with contemporaneous success as one axis and the predictor of long-term success—trust—as the other. The first question, then, was to choose a means for quantifying contemporaneous success. Survey data initially were unhelpful, due to individuals' inability to comfortably or accurately assess their own transaction history. Profitability, while compelling, is influenced by many variable factors (such as currency valuation and one-time charges) and is seldom reported on a brand-by-brand basis. Thus in its early form, the BSM measurement of "transactions" was based on market share. It was reasonably accessible and relatively stable among other external factors, such as category-wide trends. Beer and automotive come to mind, for instance. We applied the Herfindahl-

Hirschman Index, a logarithm commonly used to express market concentration, to plot brands along the x-axis.

Market share, however, presented two vexing problems. One is that reporting is inconsistent, particularly among multinational marketers, and apples were often sorted with oranges. The second was the overlap of brands and markets. For example, Whole Foods has a much larger market share in organic or specialty grocery than it does in the general grocery category. Which to apply to the brand? Conversely, national pizza chains are in the quick-serve restaurant (QSR) category but compete most intensely with other pizza chains. How to define them? Though for our purposes the x-axis was not nearly as critical as the y-axis, those overlaps led to arbitrary, unsatisfying choices. Hence we decided to divine contemporary popularity by surveying consumers on the following question and a providing slider for the response:

> When you purchase from this category, how often (what percentage of the time) do you purchase from this brand?

The answers from the survey were collected, averaged and aggregated at the brand level.

Why Ask Y?

The "trust" component, far more complex, is also derived from survey data. Typically, we use an outside research firm to survey one thousand respondents in a representative sample of the U.S. population, ages eighteen to sixty-five. After being screened for familiarity with the brand, respondents are asked to indicate their perception of the brand by reading pairs of clarifying statements and sliding a bar between the two, indicating their level of agreement. A numeric value is assigned based on where the respondents move the bar. The statements, which were refined and validated over the course of multiple surveys to ensure reliability and accuracy, assess the three critical components of trust, those Three Cs from Chapter 3: credibility, care and congruency. We then use a statistical technique common in predictive modeling called Principal Components Analysis to calculate a single numeric value to represent trust, for placement along the y-axis.

The resulting schema is both imperfect and perfectly illustrative of contemporary reality—at least in consumer marketing. But before we leave this chapter, we should consider the question of sustainability as it relates to a business-to-business company. We have previously observed that a handful of industrial juggernauts like ExxonMobil don't have to achieve enlightenment to survive; they'll do just fine on the sheer power of physical, financial and geopolitical infrastructure. That does not mean, however, that business-to-business marketers are immune to the four forces, or that they cannot benefit from Relationship Era thinking. Let's think of such an enterprise—and not just any one. It must be publicly held, unlike the "alternative marketers" that can more freely operate according to the Great Law of the Iroquois Nation, and it must be huge. So how about a Fortune 10 multinational industrial colossus that runs consumer businesses in finance and appliances, but that depends for most of its revenue on sales of industrial equipment and medical diagnostics unavailable on Amazon.com? And, for good measure, what if its business strategy were predicated on the global demand for environmental sustainability—or, at least, progress in that direction? We refer, of course, to General Electric. Can GE adapt, and should it adapt, to the Relationship Era?

The answer, of course, is yes, and it is trying, and it had better succeed.

Plant Turbines

As if this were not already abundantly clear, meeting the demands of a hyperconnected, hypertransparent world does not consist of starting a Twitter feed. Equally, matters of reputation and trust—which for a company like GE have a huge bearing on relationships with prospective industrial customers, Wall Street, public-interest groups and governments across the world—can no longer be addressed by dialing up BBDO advertising for another feel-good image campaign. We've already addressed an environmental record that follows the corporation like a bad penny. Not only has GE yet to live down the decades-long dumping of carcinogenic PCBs into the Hudson River, it continues to be among the top ten corporate air polluters in the country, and ranks fourth among all entities, public and private, in industrial contamination resulting in Superfund sites.[5] Not to mention defense contracting scandals, profit inflation and insider-trading scandals at the then-Kidder Peabody subsidiary and former CEO Jack Welch's platinum retirement parachute.

Adding economic insult to environmental injury, in 2010 GE earned $14.2 billion in profits—$5 billion from U.S. operations—yet paid no federal taxes. In fact, thanks to tax code loopholes, it got a $3.2 billion rebate.[6] Meanwhile, it has laid off five thousand workers since 2008 while dramatically increasing executive compensation. This is the sort of record that fills city parks around the world with righteous squatters from the seething 99 percent. Which, according to Beth Comstock, senior vice president and chief marketing officer, GE well understands.

"The history, the bad listening, the relationships that maybe had been part of the past and we had to open up and say, 'Yeah, that is a part, but now we are going to commit to something different in the future and hold us accountable and relevant by this standard.'"

In many ways, the earth has shifted under GE's feet. In the Jack Welch glory days—during which the company's market cap grew 4,000 percent—prosperity came via ruthless focus on profits (eighty-one thousand layoffs, underperforming managers summarily fired) and shrewd portfolio management: acquisition of high-cash flow businesses that could compete first or second in their categories, and the divesture of even profitable laggards. In those days, GE Capital rode the bubble to represent 40 percent of the parent's earnings. As somebody once said, that was then; this is now. While the financing arm of the company has righted itself, the banking crisis gutted corporate profits and CEO Jeffrey Immelt has subordinated it to other business sectors. Meanwhile, GE's industrial businesses are all faced with the emergence of existential environmental crises.

Just as the world's energy needs are exploding, so too is the over-whelming urgency of reducing carbon emissions. In that circum-stance resides paradox, irony and vast opportunity: GE, infamous polluter, makes the stuff that can create energy more efficiently. Turbines. Locomotives. Jet engines. Electrical transformers and other components of the power grid. Thus, the new core strategy: to work with customers for the creation of technology that will keep the planet lit while simultaneously trying to keep the planet alive. "Imagination at work," is what BBDO's ads say.

"It's about brand, but it was equally about making a commitment to our customers that you want to be cleaner, greener, with the products that you buy," Comstock says. "We've got to help you get there and then the underlying core of all it, that frankly has gotten lost in a lot of the conversation. This is about economic viability. It's about sustainability in its first order. If we all can't thrive economi-cally, we can never create a cleaner, greener future.

"If you've been about business, you've always been about relation-ships, but it is on all the time. Highly connected, highly transparent and open, honest discussions about value, in a way that perhaps we are just beginning to appreciate this shared purpose and value. The ecosystem—that we all have to solve these problems. We all have to benefit together."

Benefit together. Comstock has succinctly articulated the care component of trust relationships. She is very good at articulating. But can a notoriously bullying corporate leviathan such as GE truly go touchy-feely? And, more important, must it? Comstock's vision assumes that GE cannot sustain a sustainability business from any-place but the "sustainable" quadrant of the Brand Sustainability Map. Others—ExxonMobil, let's say—clearly operate under a dif-ferent calculus. In that respect, assuming this is not mere p.r. spin, GE is the canary in the coal mine of the world's industrial future.

The outcome is obviously uncertain. Equally obvious is that one of the least likely candidates for philosophical transformation has deter-mined that the Relationship Era changes everything, and is retooling its business accordingly. This to sell turbines to governments. We dare say if you sell consumer package goods to consumers, the path is clear.

6

THE SECRET SECRET

Courage is not simply one of the virtues, but the form
of every virtue at the testing point.

—C. S. LEWIS

ecret is no secret. It's been around since 1956, the first deodorant
marketed exclusively to women. Through most of its history, the
advertising themes have focused on product attributes, most famously: "Strong enough for a man, but made for a woman." In the
past twenty years, truth has increasingly validated hype, with technological advances yielding more antiperspirant efficacy with a
sheerer—and therefore more invisible—application. But throughout its history, advertising has frequently employed slice-of-life narratives getting to the consumer's confidence. With Secret, you can
be active, get nervous, wear silk, lift your arms and generally live
your life without fear of god-awful embarrassment over the fact that
like everyone else on earth, you sweat.

Product efficacy and consumer confidence. Not a bad combination.
Yet Procter began losing confidence in the relevance of the positioning.

"It was always about key issues of the day and inspiring women
to be fearless," says Kevin Hochman, brand manager for skin care

and personal care at Procter & Gamble North America. But some-how, around late 2004, the brand stewards sensed that the theme was getting dated. "We walked away," Hochman says. "We thought, women *are* empowered and maybe this isn't so relevant. That was a mistake."

It was especially ill timed, as the all-natural trend left some younger women gravitating away from aluminum-based antiperspi-rants and toward body sprays and body washes. As Secret's growth flattened, the marketer focused ever more on the product's attri-butes and ever less on the underlying brand promise of underarm empowerment. One 2006 campaign asked women to divulge se-crets on the Web ("My fiancé thinks I'm eight years younger than I actually am.") And even when "confidence" was the theme of a typical Procter & Gamble slice-of-life commercial—as it was when the "clinical-strength" line extension was launched in 2007—the confidence was juxtaposed against shame. Yeah, the happy bride is dancing uninhibitedly at her wedding, her arms raised above her. But the poor bridesmaids are afraid to even reach for the tossed bridal bouquet, lest their soggy pits be exposed. This ad wasn't made in 1966. It aired in 2007. (The breakthrough, such that it was, came with the first images in American advertising of actual underarm sweat. Somehow the republic survived.)

Through 2008, the novelty of "clinical-strength" Secret helped boost the brand, but within a year or so that effect eventually waned. The new segment was very expensive and the economy was getting very bad. But in two other respects, the timing was most propitious. For one thing, top management were beginning to loudly voice con-fidence in the power and inevitability of purpose-driven marketing. "We expect every one of our brands to be guided by a purpose that defines how it uniquely touches and improves lives," Marc Pritchard, global marketing and brand building officer, declared to the Asso-ciation of National Advertisers. "We think of it as the soul of the brand."[1]

Pritchard's thinking bears more than a passing mention here, because his is not a privately held business populated entirely by true believers fresh out of a Save Our Rainforests protest or Burning Man. It is the largest advertiser in the world with a market cap of $175 billion and twenty-four $1 billion-plus brands. It is conservative in all it does. Operating from purpose, Prichard told his colleagues,

> can open up new possibilities to deliver that benefit to consumers. It means shifting our mindset from marketing to serving. That means changing from marketing *to* people (so we get them to do what we want them to do, which is buy our products) to *serving* people with our brands to make their lives better. And that can take many forms. Of course, it's better products, but it's also non-product services. It's entertainment that brings people together and it's acts of kindness and generosity that [make] them part of the larger community.

Purpose "also means thinking of who we serve as people. Now this may seem obvious, but when we have a mind-set of marketing to consumers, it leads to a focus of getting them to try to do what we want them to do: consume our products. But, when we focus on serving people, we're forced to gain a deeper understanding about their whole life and give them what they want to make their entire life better. And when we focus on serving people, we uncover human insights—not product insights. Deep human insights that define the essence of human behavior. They represent universal human truths, motivations and tensions that must be solved by the benefits of our brands.

"And from these insights," he added, very significantly, "we create big ideas."[2]

Bomb the Ban

Big ideas. Hold that thought, will you? Meantime, suffice it to say that at Doug's agency, MEplusYOU, no proclamation from client management had ever sounded quite so sweet. What Pritchard was espousing was the core belief of the agency—the purpose proposition, more or less, of MEplusYOU itself. Let us just say that the agency worked very diligently with Secret, for which it had long done digital work, to turn a corporate proclamation into reality. Now, of course, when you're speaking of what marketing people refer to as "low-involvement" products and try to imbue them with some larger significance, you get into some awkward territory. Yeah, sure, Harley-Davidson. Whole Foods. Patagonia. Plenty of room for passion there. But what about categories that aren't so emotionally charged? Try plumbing the depths of a deodorant, looking for inspiration in perspiration. It sounds like a scene from a movie satirizing advertising.

In point of fact, it *is* a scene from a movie satirizing advertising. One of the more hilarious moments in our friend Morgan Spurlock's 2011 film *POM Wonderful Presents: The Greatest Movie Ever Sold* came when the brand management team for Ban Roll-On is asked what the brand is about. "What are the words you would use to describe Ban?" he inquires. "Ban is . . . ?" What follows is a very long, very embarrassing pause. It was not meant to be a trick question, but the silence speaks volumes as the Banistas struggle to fill in the blank. Movie theaters fill with gathering laughter. Then, after what seems an eternity, a Ban manager offers, "It's about superior technology."

All right, that's an answer. Not a great one, but a valid one. Then Spurlock retorts, "Technology's not the way you wanna describe something somebody's putting in their armpit," and that line brings down the house.[3]

Surely if you polled these same audiences and asked them about "brand purpose," many would roll their eyes at what seems like the most ludicrously tortured corporate-speak. Yet the tension and humor of the Ban-Spurlock exchange don't flow from any absurdity in asking what the brand means. On the contrary, the joke hinges on the public's visceral understanding that brand stewards should be working at a minimum with a sense of why they are in business. The viewers weren't laughing at the notion of brand ethos. They were laughing at Ban for not having one.

Secret does. The brand articulated it, as a matter of fact, not long before Spurlock began filming. And it did so by understanding the brand not just in the realm of stained blouses, but in a woman's life writ large:

> We believe in the equality of the genders and that all people should be able to pursue their goals without fear. We believe that by acting courageously, supporting others, empathizing with their challenges, and finding innovative solutions, we can help women to be more fearless.

At MEplusYOU—having participated in the discovery process run by BrightHouse Consulting that led to this proclamation—the Secret account team spent months debating how to help the client express and achieve its stated beliefs. There was no brief, per se, nor even any specific guidance about how to go about making the agency's efforts conform to the philosophical vision. But one major element loomed large. The purpose work was completed in January 2009. In thirteen months would commence the 2010 Winter Olympic Games in Vancouver and Procter & Gamble had negotiated a $10 million sponsorship with the U.S. Olympic Committee[4] (a precursor to an eight-year worldwide partnership with the International Olympic Committee beginning in 2012),[5] its first ever Olympics investment. Everyone was wracking their brains to come up with a memorable, relevant, impactful and efficient way to exploit this opportunity.

At one of our general briefings, the team learned, more or less as an aside, that an endorser for P&G's beauty products, downhill skier Lindsey Vonn, was also a ski jumper—an event not sanctioned for women in the Winter Games. Lindsey wanted to compete, but for some anachronistic reason attributable to paternalism, sexism, bureaucracy, inertia or whatever, was barred from doing so. All bundled up, you might say, but no place to soar. Among the many ideas to be dry markered to the whiteboard in MEplusYOU's conference room was the notion of supporting an extremely popular P&G spokes-athlete in her bid to jump.

Damn You, Google Search!

Alas, the ski-jumping deliberations were all based on a false premise. It turned out that a routine Google search for Lindsey Vonn—who is not a ski jumper—also returned results for Lindsey Van, who is. Van, alas, was not a P&G endorser. The account team had the right kind of thinking, but the wrong kind of Lindsey. Still, the idea of supporting women ski jumpers seemed intriguing. Along with ten other ideas, it lingered in the agency's collective consciousness. Not long after, the client convened a Chicago summit of its many agencies along with a delegation from Facebook to brainstorm ways to integrate ongoing initiatives with social media—specifically, to give people more reasons to care, and to share. Kristi Maynor and Leslie Shaffer of MEplusYOU were present and very much paying attention. They left the all-day affair and headed for O'Hare Airport, going back and forth on what might constitute a core creative idea to integrate on Facebook with the brand's core values. On that forty-minute journey from the Leo Burnett offices on West Wacker Drive, they picked up on the subject of Lindsey "not Vonn" Van. If supporting the basic equity of elite female athletes performing event for event alongside of elite men wasn't something women could rally around, nothing was. For Leslie, everything coalesced. *All people should be able to pursue their goals without fear.* But of course! Dragging her roller board down the aisle of the MD-80, she swiveled her head back to Kristi and announced: "I want a billboard that says 'Let her jump!'"

What followed at MEplusYOU was what you call "total buy in." This was followed by near-total buy in at Secret brand management, which proceeded enthusiastically but not incautiously. Brand manager Jason Duff did not write a blank check, but funded the video that would be the core element of the initiative. Later, when

Jason showed it to his wife, she cried—a reaction that helped embolden him to spend enough money to call attention to a "Let Her Jump!" Facebook page hosting the video. Some seeding money was spent to place the video on key blogs. Banners were purchased adjacent to YouTube sports channels and on Facebook. Total cost: $300,000, or about half the tab for making—never mind airing—a single TV spot. The client also changed the package of Secret Clinical Sport, previously featuring a woman boxer, to depict a woman skier.

Over the next six months—including the ten February days of the Vancouver games—three things happened. First, more than seven hundred thousand people viewed the video. Second, sales of Secret spiked like crazy.

"This was the first time we could pinpoint that activating against purpose generated a huge sales lift," Hochman says. "We saw the Clinical Sport SKU up 85 percent during the Olympics, and the entire Clinical line-up saw growth in the teens. Last fiscal year, the Clinical family grew nearly 20 percent in sales. Pretty cool."

Oh, and one other thing. In April 2011, the International Olympic Committee decided to include ski jumping for women in the 2014 Winter Games.[6]

But Wait . . .

There's more.

In the summer of 2010, P&G's Kevin Hochman became increasingly intrigued by the experiential marketing philosophy of a restaurant on Madison Road in Cincinnati called Boca. Staff there was inculcated with the mantra "BPA"—short for blow people away. Employees were charged with making the entire experience memorable, and the strategy is availing still today. Here is one of many recent Yelp comments for the restaurant:

> If I could give Boca 10 stars, I would. We had the most incredible dining experience EVER last night at Boca. We have eaten in

many great restaurants all over the world, and I would put Boca up against any of them as the most amazing meal.[7]

Hochman believed there was nothing about BPA that couldn't apply to a packaged good, as long as all involved did not view their relationship with the end user as merely the delivery of a satisfactory product at a price, but rather a 360-degree enterprise informing every interaction with everyone along the line.

Once again, at MEplusYOU, where the Relationship Era is literally a trademark, this was right in the agency sweet spot. Matt Whitaker, VP for strategy, put together some ideas in a PowerPoint presentation. Meanwhile, in Cincinnati, Secret associate brand manager Matt Hollenkamp had heard from the BrightHouse agency in Atlanta about a remarkable emerging story. Olympic medalist Diana Nyad, at the age of 60, was preparing to swim the 103 miles of open ocean between Havana, Cuba, and Miami. BrightHouse had connections to her people; was this something Secret could associate with?

Well, yes. "Female fearlessness," after all. Not to mention that one of the newer items in the Secret Clinical line was a waterproof deodorant designed specifically for swimming. All the team had to do was negotiate a sponsorship, develop a Facebook presence and visual identities for garments and gear, decals for the accompanying fleet of boats and kayaks and other signage.

All within one week, because Diana was preparing to begin the swim in seven days.

Before the first day was out, the agency was on the ground at her California home shooting three promotional videos. Everything else moved along at an equally breakneck pace and miraculously, just in the nick of time, Secret was in place as an official sponsor of this inspiring effort to conquer the limits of nature, age, human endurance and any residual questions about the fitness of women to be icons of fitness. Then Diana postponed the swim. Heavy seas and visa complications with the Castro government forced the delay. Then more delay, and more. This went on for six weeks until Diana—with hurricane season upon her—was forced to postpone her historic effort until the following year. This gave the agency a chance to catch its breath (and to fulfill the growing demand for promotional swag). It also gave the world a chance to take notice.

Water Proof

The world did. The site, which with the luxury of time was updated with a video of Diana speaking in her own words about her plans, was inundated with the encouragement of well-wishers, who over the course of a year were able to follow the progress of preparations for the historic swim. On August 7, 2011, in Havana's Marina Hemingway—with wind conditions and water temperatures ideal—it finally began. Escorted by a flotilla of press, medical personnel and a thirty-person crew, Nyad took to the south Atlantic on what proved to be a doomed journey. Within three hours, she injured a shoulder, but swam through the pain in strong ocean currents that pushed her miles off course. Though kayakers paddled ahead of her with electronic shark repellant, this was no protection against box jellyfish; their repeated stings compromised her respiratory system, triggering asthma attacks. She still pressed on for twenty-nine hours. Finally, breathing difficulties forced her out of the water. Compromised almost from the beginning she nonetheless had swum half the distance to Florida.

"You have to live your life with passion," she told the press afterward. "You show your will, you feel proud of yourself when you go to bed at night."[8]

Her passion was not in question. Less than seven weeks later, the sixty-two-year-old tried again. In that attempt, she swam forty-nine miles in forty hours—pestered by barracuda and shark—before stings from man-o'-war jellyfish put her at risk of anaphylactic shock.[9] A third attempt in August 2012 ended prematurely, as well, for identical reasons.[10] Nyad had not conquered the Florida Straits, but she had won the respect of millions. Among them were those who followed intently on Secret's dedicated Facebook page. At the risk of seeming vulgar, it bears noting that before Diana even dove in the water, sales of Secret Clinical Strength Waterproof, the most expensive product in the Secret line, doubled. Some of this lift can be attributed, of course, to the most rudimentary aspects of brand aware-ness. And, of course, there are the benefits of borrowed interest when famous names are bought and paid for. But, absent a mammoth ad-vertising expenditure, never a *doubling*. The only explanation for what occurred with the brand is the notion of membership: women inspired by Diana Nyad's efforts wished to be associated with a brand operating under the same set of beliefs. Perhaps they sensed the difference between the venality of so many cynical, one-off pro-motions and the authenticity of Secret's motives. In short, they wished to embrace a fellow traveler in the struggle.

Lest we be too dismissive of "one-off" initiatives, we must ac-knowledge that both "Let Her Jump" and Diana Nyad's swims were finite propositions. And they were, naturally, opportunistic—which is either a compliment or an epithet, depending on the motives and conduct of the parties involved. It's not difficult, however, to iden-tify the difference; there are questions for marketers to ask them-selves when such opportunities arise:

> Does the effort exploit the plight of the subjects at the center of the initiative?

> Does the marketing material cheaply exploit the emotions of the target audience?

> Is the association between the brand and its third-party beneficiary genuine, or nakedly transactional?

> Does the effort conform with the stated or implicit purpose of the brand?

Clearly, Secret passes the, ahem, smell test on all counts. The swims were not stunts, they did not prey cynically on emotions or misfortune and Secret's connection was a direct expression of its brand purpose. In all, you might say, a perfect relationship.

The Bully Pulpit

Let's speak a bit more about opportunism. It is obvious that, ideally, a brand wishes to acquire users early, and keep them for a lifetime. So it is equally obvious that Procter & Gamble benefits if it attracts young girls to Secret at the moment of adolescence, and heaven knows there is no shortage of advertising ways—online, off-line and mobile—to help achieve the goal. Secret, no less than any brand, avails itself of all appropriate channels to reach its prospects. But more than other brands, Secret knows what it is about; it is about fearlessness, a purpose that, as we've seen, informs its every move. Whereupon the question becomes "What instills fear in young girls?" The answer to which requires zero research: the judgment, actual or imagined, of their peers. Social anxiety and bullying are the vicious cycle that can turn the last days of childhood into a daily hell.

At lead Secret agency Leo Burnett, addressing adolescent meanness had been batted around for more than a year, an emotion-laden idea in search of a business rationale. After the impact of "Let Her Jump" and Diana Nyad made more tangible the theoretical underpinnings of purpose-driven initiatives, brand management was emboldened to activate the program dubbed "Mean Stinks." The idea was to help kids be civil, encouraging, supportive and kind instead of little savages making one another miserable for perceived social gain or sport. The Facebook page would be a forum for conflict resolution—in the form of apology—and generally provide safe haven from the angst of seventh grade.

The Mean Stinks Facebook page launched in January 2011, with the support of ads on Facebook itself, asking young teens to apologize for bullying they may have inflicted on their peers. Now, anyone who has ever endured the *Lord of the Flies* realities of middle school might assume this kind of exercise would itself become a target of ridicule. Nope. Through Mean Stinks, in the space of a few weeks, 75,000 kids sent apologies to their peers or posted friendly graffiti. With the help of the Facebook ads, on February 10, 2011,

Mean Stinks and the Secret page drew 203,000 new fans in one day. The activity triggered 339,000 text and video engagements and yielded 1.3 million placements in the newsfeeds of the fans' Friends.[11]

We offer those statistics with full knowledge that depending on your viewpoint they are either impressive or—if you're accustomed to buying audiences by the millions upon millions—pitiful. Well, we possess no magical quantifying metric, but we can say categorically that pitiful the numbers are not. These are not 339,000 Facebookers who passively encountered an ad. These are 339,000 who took some action to further engage with Secret, many of whom explicitly expressed solidarity with Secret's efforts. Over time, by virtue of the inherently exponential dynamics of word of mouth, those numbers will grow. And each individual represents not an audience member who may or may not have registered an ad message, remembered the ad message, liked the ad message, believed the ad message, cared about the ad message, snorted derisively at the ad message or perhaps actively avoided the ad message but rather someone who positively affirmed a shared belief.

Also, says P&G's Hochman, "In the fiscal year that Mean Stinks launched, total brand dollar share was up 8 percent. Our Clinical family of SKUs, which were the products associated with Mean Stinks, grew 20 percent in volume versus the previous year. On our Facebook page, we saw fan engagement increase 24× with the launch of Mean Stinks, and about half of those fans engage with the page on a regular basis."

So effective has been Mean Stinks that in February 2012, it was cited by Facebook in its initial public offering as evidence of marketing efficacy.[12] The IPO resulted in a $100 billion valuation for the company.[13] (That value has since been halved, based on what Facebook *hasn't* been able to prove to the market: its potential as an advertising medium.)

On that day, Burnett and MEplusYOU basked in the glow of positivity from what the press called the "Mean Stinks campaign." The terminology, however, made us wince. We do not view these efforts as *campaigns*, a term that implies not only a time limit, but a martial sense of seeking to conquer an army of consumers. We call them ignitions, sparking the interests of like-minded people in a common cause. Long after a typical campaign might have run its course—leaving the brand managers approximately right where they started—the Secret community will still be a living, breathing and almost certainly growing crowd.

Including, not incidentally, the Secret community within P&G, where Hochman says a sense of fearlessness also has taken hold.

"The way the Secret team operates now, compared to the way they operated three years ago, it's like day and night," he says. "And when people are living the brand, they're more excited to come to work, with more pep in their step. It's just much more enabling and inspiring."

Inspiration about perspiration? Not exactly, but surely about doing something more satisfying than pushing products into the faceless marketplace. Hochman's enthusiasm about his team's enthusiasm brings to mind the eloquent observation of twentieth-century French writer and aviator Antoine de Saint-Exupéry: "If you want to build a ship, don't herd people together to collect wood. And don't assign them tasks and work. But, rather, teach them to long for the endless immensity of the sea."

7

THAT THING CALLED LIKE

The single most important decision any of us will ever make is whether or not to believe the universe is friendly.

— *ALBERT EINSTEIN*

In May of 2011, Lior and Vardit Adler had a baby girl. They announced the joyous event on Facebook, which is what people do. Maybe you get more cute onesies and rattles in the mail if you send out baby announcements on nice card stock in actual envelopes, but if your goal is pure information delivery to your social circles, Facebook is definitely the way to go. You also get immediate gratification. The Adlers' Facebook friends roster is just above one hundred yet they immediately received forty Likes.

Forty-one, actually. Because that's also what they named the child.

Like. In honor of the button.

The Adlers really like the Like button, and they liked the idea of fashioning its like in the, like, flesh-and-blood world. "We named her Like because it's modern and innovative," her mom, Vardit, told the newspaper *Maariv*. "I checked that the name does not exist elsewhere in the country; that was the main condition for me." So perhaps, somewhere in Tel Aviv, Poke and Wall were taken. The gesture, in any event, was polarizing. Some smiled, and some cringed at the implications of consigning a child to life as a verb. It's worth noting, however, that while Facebook terms of service prohibit an infant having her own user page, there is now a Like Adler community—and 5,858 people like it. *Oy vey.* But let's put aside the question of whether such iconoclastic naming is an act of benevolent parents. (The couple has another daughter named Pie.) And let's just for a moment put aside the fact that Jewish tradition requires naming children after the dead. Can we just agree that this simple, virtual device, the button itself, has after only three years insinuated itself remarkably into modern culture?

Rhetorical question. According to a 2012 white paper published by ExactTarget, the Indianapolis consultancy, 93 percent of all regular Facebook users click on Like at least once a month.[1] That percentage, depending on which definition of "regular user" one subscribes to, includes just shy of one billion human souls who engage in a behavior that in 2009 did not exist. They Like content within Facebook—wall comments and posts by their friends, for instance—and they Like content distributed throughout the entirety of the World Wide Web—an article on the *Huffington Post,* let's say. "Dead Man Found in Foreclosed Home as Much as Four Years Later" was Liked 1,039 times in the first 24 hours. Yet that expression of fondness is a drop in the bucket compared to, for example, the Coca-Cola fan page.

Let's just think about Coca-Cola, a product that is not good for you but which is nonetheless the most well-known and among the most cherished in the world. Its Facebook page was actually launched in 2008, not by anybody in the company but by a pair of genuine admirers, Californians Michael Jedrzejewski and Dusty Sorg.[2] They wanted to because, in their eyes, the handful of then-existing Coke pages were too flimsy and amateurish for so iconic a brand. "It's not just a consumer product," Jedrzejewski says. "It's almost something that permeates your subconscious. It's this simple indulgence that has touched almost everybody on earth."

Their effort featured a dramatic, high-resolution photo of a Coke bottle and a summary of corporate history borrowed from Wikipedia. The page went up in September, says Jedrzejewski, "and when we checked in three weeks or a month later it had just about 700,000 fans." And from those fans all kinds of tributes: songs, videos, photos, poems, you name it. A composer named John Griffin posted, "I love Coke so much I wrote a few jingles!" One went like this:

> You've a Coca-Cola cra-ving. It's callin' your name.
> Pick up the phone, and thanks for drinkin' Coke.

Pick up the phone? Whatever. Jedrzejewski's favorite of all the countless items posted over four years was a sort of junior high school Parkour video put together in May 2009 by Jason and Neal, a pair of teenage American expats in Santiago, Dominican Republic. The joke is they're bored and thirsty, so they agree to go out for a Coke. This involves five hair-raising minutes of reckless climbing and jumping at great heights, plus a run through some jungle. Then back home, where they throw themselves exhausted into their chairs, sucking down the last of their drinks. Then the kicker: they're still thirsty. So, off they go again.

Yes, they so love their Coke that they risked breaking their necks. Jedrzejewski and Sorg, at least, confined their passion to some spirited clicking.

"It was an effortless thing," Jedrzejewski says. "We made a page. The page stuck."

The Virtual Country That Refreshes

Not, however, the ownership. In 2010, for fear of third parties with less benevolent intent hijacking brand names, Facebook changed its terms of service to demand that companies host their own fan pages—whereupon Coca-Cola assumed control of the e-shrine and its then millions of fans. It did so in full collaboration with the founders, which was kind of like recruiting groupies to write songs for the band. The partnership of one struggling screenwriter and his struggling actor pal with one of the largest industrial corporations in the world has gone fairly well. The Coca-Cola Facebook page now has more than forty-five million fans. Forty-five million people(!), aggregated via the Like button and its "Become a Fan" predecessor, all in the space of five years. Forty-five million people is not a social circle. That is Ukraine. Just to put that in perspective, the cost of reaching the equivalent audience with TV advertising—one commercial aired once—is about $1 million. Coca-Cola has access to the audience 24/7, for free.

"You begin to look at it as an entirely new media channel," says Michael Donnelly, who when we spoke to him was director of worldwide interactive marketing for Coca-Cola. "From a media perspective there is great value in the overall impressions." Yet Coca-Cola seldom uses the connection with this captive and clearly receptive audience to deliver anything resembling an ad. "An awful lot of our strategy is baked into seeing and observing and watching why people assemble around the brand in the first place," Donnelly says, "and in almost every single case, it's not to have our advertising blasted at them. So we've got a very different approach than most brands. . . . It is very much about celebrating people's individual passion for the brand and their manifestations of their passion."

These manifestations manifest in two ways. Some simply come in over the virtual transom, the songs, videos and love notes of all shapes and sizes. The second source of fan content comes in response to postings from the brand itself. Just as you might add a comment to a Little League home-run video posted by your BFF, Coke fans weigh in on content offered by the brand.

"If we were to put a post out there to ask a simple question—'If you were to share a Coke today with someone famous, who would it be?'—I can tell you that we've many times exceeded ten thousand comments where people respond back, and an equal amount of Likes. We might get up to twenty thousand pieces of engagement to a simple post like that. And generally 90 percent of them are within the first few minutes or within the first hour."

Consider the experience of Coke's "Happiness Machine." Donnelly's people placed a new Coke vending machine against the wall of a freshly constructed secret room at St. John's University on Long Island, New York. When students deposited money for a Coke, sometimes the machine dispensed two Cokes. Sometimes sixteen Cokes. Sometimes bouquets of flowers. A pepperoni pizza. A six-foot-long sub. All were being fed by a Coke employee hidden behind the wall, but to the students it was just a hilarious surprise. We know this because a camera captured the whole deal, and the footage was edited into a YouTube video. Coca-Cola introduced that video on January 1, 2011, with a one-line status update on its Facebook page. A year later, the video had amassed fifteen thousand-plus Likes and four million views.

Though the brand continues to buy impressions by the billions with advertising around the world, Donnelly says, "The level of expressions or engagement we generally see is far more valuable. So we are looking very hard at the level of engagement it takes to Like a brand, the level of engagement it takes to upload a picture, the level of engagement it takes to actually produce a video and put it up, and then developing strategies to drive more of those individual tactics that people are doing in support of the brand."

On the day this paragraph was written, the brand was supported by thousands of wall posts, including a shout-out from Indonesia (*a=Every nation know what they want to drink. The answer is :always coca cola :),* a request for more variety in packaging (*Bring 500 ml and 2 L Diet Coke to China, NOW!*) and, from England, one handsome line drawing of the late Kim Jong Il crushing a Diet Coke can in his iron fist.

"Something that astonishes me every day," Donnelly says, "is the great length people go to, to create things that are somehow relevant or very centric to this brand—the incredible passion, or loyalty, or just what drives someone to make an incredible, well-produced video about them and this brand. And then even more specifically it astonishes me every day as to what they do with it. Because them posting it to the page isn't giving it to Coca-Cola; it's actually giving it to the community and sharing it amongst people like themselves."

Coca-Cola has more reason than most to understand why. The annals of marketing record that, long before social media, the world discovered that consumers feel a proprietary stake in brands. This was made apparent in 1985 when the Coca-Cola Company unilaterally decided to change the formula of Coca-Cola. After a century using the recipe called Merchandise 7X, management felt the need to sweeten Coke, the better to fend off encroachment by rival Pepsi in the United States. Naturally, they did consumer research border to border, coast to coast, and in blind taste tests the new formula was the clear favorite. Unfortunately, they asked the wrong question. The question they asked was "Do you prefer cup A or cup B?" The question they should have asked was "Do you want us fucking with the flavor of Coke?"

The answer, it turned out, was an overwhelming No! Consumers wigged out, and Coke was forced into one of the most humiliating reversals in marketing history.[3]

Yet, according to Joe Tripodi, Coca-Cola's CMO, the notion of being owned by your consumers still needed to be hammered home. That occurred in 2006, when a group called EeepyBird.com posted a YouTube video showing four Mentos candies being put into a two-liter bottle of Diet Coke, yielding an astonishing eruption, a soft-drink geyser. One of the earliest viral videos, it has been viewed more than fifteen million times.

"There was hysteria over that," Tripodi told us. "'How could they do that with our brand!?' And then people realized, 'Well, gee, that's what consumers want to do.'" That realization, he says, informs the company's social strategy to this day. "You know what? We don't own the brand. The people who use our product own the brand. Let them talk about the brand for us.

"I used to think that loyalty was the top of that pyramid: awareness, consideration, preference, loyalty. Then I said, 'Oh my God, advocacy is the bigger thing.' If you can get people to be active advocates as opposed to passive loyalists, I think [that] is so much a part of our future."

Which is why, in one important respect, Facebook interactions are worth more than the equivalent number of ad impressions.

Engagement, by definition, is active. It is also charged with positive sentiment—sentiment that boasts far more authenticity than any claim of "happiness" propagated at extremely great expense by the brand itself. It is, you might say, "The Real Thing." And, of course, nobody has barged into anybody's private space to make it all happen. On the contrary, Likers seek you out. Whether we're speaking of a popular brand or a weird *HuffPo* slice-of-death story, the fact is a significant number of individuals with plenty of other things to do take the positive step of moving their cursor and clicking to register approval. The question is, as the number and growth of Likes are increasingly cited by brands, media and other institutions as evidence of consumer engagement, "What exactly does that approval mean?"

My Name's Everyman; I Carry a Badge

The answer begins with understanding why—digitally or otherwise—people feel compelled to volunteer their taste in soft drinks, pulp nonfiction, movies, restaurants and virtually every other human artifact including, it turns out, newborn Israelis. Why do we wear heavily branded garments—whether a Hermes bag or a Nike T-shirt? Why do we list our favorite movies, books and TV shows on our Facebook pages? Why do we belly up to the bar and loudly order Tito's or Ketel One when Grey Goose or probably Ambassador is virtually indistinguishable? Why do we decorate our dorm rooms with posters of rockers and reproductions of famous artworks? Why do we deface our automobiles with bumper stickers announcing our media choices or our politics, and the rear windows with college decals? Not to mention vanity license plates. (MY-BENZ. Well, aren't *you* special?)

This phenomenon is what social scientists call "badging" or "self-presentation," wherein a person endeavors to define himself in varying degrees of conspicuousness for the benefit of the outside world. As University of London professor Celia Lury wrote in her 1996 book *Consumer Culture*, "One of the most important ways in which people relate to each other socially is through the mediation of things."[4] Scholars Helga Dittmar and Lucy Pepper called such displays "tangible symbols of identity."[5] We are what we enjoy, we are what we believe, and we are very much—at least in our own minds— what we buy. This central fact is red meat for the most strident critics of the consumer culture, for when taken to its logical conclusion such preening leads to wanton consumption of finite resources, the devaluation of human qualities and arguably, ultimately, a sort of moral vacuum cloaked in a superficial layer of mere things. Your authors hereby stipulate the dangers and general obnoxiousness of mindless acquisitiveness, but we by no means abhor the very human nature of self-presentation. For starters, denying human nature is a low-percentage proposition. Secondly, badging is extremely convenient. As anyone who ever picked up a blind date can tell you, a quick scan at the bookshelf, CD rack and décor offers volumes of information that Aunt Hildegard, bless her busybody soul, might have left out. Relationships are built on commonality, and that *Best of Vanilla Ice* CD can be a deal killer. (Or, we must concede, the beginning of a beautiful friendship.) And what is true in the living room is no less true online. Facebook is the bookshelf scan times 850 million 24/7.

The implications for self-presentation online were recognized by academicians at an early stage of the Web. While Mark Zuckerberg was still a faceless Harvard freshman, professors Hope J. Schau of the University of Arizona and Mary C. Gilly of the University of California, Irvine, anticipated hyper-badging in a journal article titled "We Are What We Post?" Online as in real life, they concluded, individuals "use brands as shorthand for describing to others who they are, as well as who they are not." But unlike the physical world, where badging generally necessitates actually possessing the goods in question, the online space permits you to be conspicuously hypothetical:

> For example, consumers may feel Gucci expresses their identities but be unable to own Gucci items in [real life]. In personal Web space, consumers' brand associations are limited only by their

imaginations and computer skills. They can literally associate themselves with any brand by digital appropriation and manipulation of digital symbols. Interestingly, our informants demonstrate a harmonious reliance on self-presentation strategies that in some way reflect the material real.

Furthermore, you don't need Aunt Hildegard luring anyone into your apartment.

In cyberspace, meaning is communicated far beyond the people in proximity to the communicator; instead, the world is watching. The underlying assumption is that, by studying people's possession portfolios, others gain access to the possessor's intangible self.[6]

Expression of self is not the only instinctual aspect of Liking. Another is the human imperative to share, and it's easy to understand why that is hardwired; families and communities cannot thrive without it. But this behavior goes beyond mutual sustenance. According to psychology professor Samuel D. Gosling of the University of Texas, Like clicking exemplifies not just sharing but also the *display* of sharing. Sound primitive? Exactly.

At the Risk of Nitpicking

"There's a very good parallel for this information," Gosling says. "Primates will groom each other and they will groom each other much more than they strictly need to from a health perspective. Because what they're doing when they're grooming each other, picking the fleas or whatever from one another's coat, they're just doing it in a public way saying 'we are connected and others can see that we are connected and that we are friends, right?'"

A common human manifestation of this, Gosling says, is when friends or acquaintances fuss extravagantly about one another's appearance or recent purchase. "You know, when a group of people meet and they start cooing to each other. Like, 'Oooh, I like your shoes!' or 'Oh, your hair's so nice! Now you've cut your fringe!' It's ostensibly about the shoes, or the hair, or the football game last night. That's what it seems to be like if you looked at the content. But really, that's not what's going on at all. It's about the social act of maintaining and strengthening those social bonds." A behavior for which the Like button is tailor-made.

"It's not really about what people are saying. What it's about is saying 'Hey, I like you, you like me, we're all friends. So should the time come, we can rely on each other.' And I think really that clicking a Like in order to maintain social contact is very, very similar, it's almost equivalent, to picking the fleas out of one another's hair."

Even when social bonds are weaker and the stakes are lower, he says, the Like affirmation is mutually reassuring. "It's just a very casual, gentle way of saying, 'Hey, I'm paying attention.' I don't have to do it regularly, but we are part of the same group and should we need each other. We're all together." You posted that *HuffPo* article about the dead guy in the foreclosed house? Here's a Like for you, because, by golly, I care.

The anthro-socio-psycho-logy is compelling. If we can assume, however, that the human animal didn't actually require any new channels for displaying its humanity to retain its humanity, then who really benefits from such channels existing? The answer, first and foremost, is Facebook. Before Like was introduced, Facebook's recommendation function was a much more limited option to "Become a fan"—an action requiring more emotion and presumably more commitment than the transitory expression of approval of a single item of content. Like was meant to vastly increase the activity by lowering the threshold of admiration, and it worked.

Your Basic Win-Win-Win-Win

"They [Facebook] will tell you that [the Like button was designed] to increase the number of connections made across the site," says Jeffrey Rohrs of the Indianapolis consultancy ExactTarget, which prepared a 2012 white paper titled *The Meaning of Like*. "They would represent this altruistic angle to it," he says, "and there certainly is; they want to amplify what their users would want to amplify. But the business purpose underpinning it was to make Like a de facto button across millions of websites and blogs and e-commerce websites. And instantaneously you now had all of these sites essentially promoting Facebook interactions at no cost to Facebook. So if you look at the top retailers and their sites, five years ago there was no Like button next to that pair of pants that you wanted to buy. Now there is. And again, that comes at no cost to Facebook and it promotes the network, it promotes interactions, it increases their visibility and therefore the growth of that social network."

Twice as many people have clicked Like than those who clicked "Become a fan." This means the metadata pouring into Facebook about individual users is for the benefit of advertisers that have flocked to Facebook's way. In 2011, according to eMarketer, Facebook accounted for one in seven of all display pages on the Internet. For 2012, it was estimated to be one in five. Before the Like button was introduced in 2010, Facebook accounted for but one in fifty online ad pages. That's why hedge fund manager turned author Andy Kessler has called the Like button "one of the most valuable innovations in technology over the last several decades."[7] In that trove of metadata, after all, lies more than demographics and generalized interests; it includes specifics about sentiment and gigantic clues about intent. It's an "emotional sensor," Kessler believes, because "Advertising's nirvana is an ad chosen especially for you."[8]

Nirvana? Maybe. Maybe not. In the wake of its lucrative and historic IPO, Facebook came under close scrutiny for its potential as an ad platform—and did not fare well. The collapse of the share price in the weeks after the company went public was attributed largely to skepticism over that very issue. That skepticism only grew when General Motors canceled a $10 million Facebook ad buy on the grounds of dubious efficacy.

Yet even without the promise of ultratargeted advertising, simply as a consequence of the button's rapid ubiquity, Like benefits brand marketers. The Like widget doesn't cost them anything, either, and each time it is clicked their brand is displayed to the social circle (or a portion of it) of the one who clicks. Those impressions add up. And sometimes they add up to substantial community assembled around the brand.

No wonder, then, that in a Relationship Era placing so much stock in consumer engagement, the Facebook Like seems like a plausible—if not ideal—unit of currency. It's spontaneous. It's voluntary. It's at least minimally enthusiastic. It's ubiquitous. And, for many users, it constitutes permission to take the fledgling relationship forward. Like the dating rules at Oberlin College, it seems to say, "Yes, you may kiss me." Although what exactly it gives license for, says ExactTarget VP of marketing Rohrs, is not altogether clear.

On the Other Hand . . .

"One of the most telling statistics that we came up with," Rohrs says, "was we asked people, 'When you click that Like button on a company's Facebook page, does that actually give them permission then to market to you through Facebook?' And our expectation was that most people would say 'yes.' What was interesting is, only 15 percent told us that that always means folks can market to us. Another 46 percent said 'depends on context, sometimes they can.' But 39 percent of the people who actually are saying 'I click on the Like button' said that never means that brands should be able to market to me on Facebook. So there's this really interesting divide with almost half the audience on Facebook not thinking that these Likes should be used for marketing purposes."[9]

Never mind Oberlin; it's sixth grade. Maybe these folks Like you, but they don't *like* Like you.

Complicating matters further is the internal Facebook algorithm called EdgeRank, software that acts as triage nurse to every user's Facebook feed. Just as gunshot wounds and heart attacks get seen in the ER before broken arms and bronchitis, posts from Friends and Liked brands do not show up on your individual news feed or Timeline on a first-come, first-served basis. Priority is given to Friends and brands you've a history of most interacting with, so if you haven't spent much time sharing with Ted, the guy in your Spanish II class in high school who Friended you four years ago leading to three reunion-related messages in 2010 and nothing since, Ted's shared content will be de-prioritized and possibly squeezed out of your feed altogether. A second level of priority is given to richer content. So a Like is worth less than a comment, and a comment is worth less than a YouTube video and so on. None of which recommends a brand that you haven't much engaged with lately. Coke could send a shout-out to its forty-five million fans (or not fans) but that doesn't mean forty-five million people will see it.

Of course, Facebook supplies marketers with fairly granular analytics about actual engagement. Likes are broken down by age, gender, location and language, and by rudimentary approximations of reach and frequency, along mass-media lines. Brands can see the total number of potential impressions (Likes × the number of Likers' friends); the raw numbers of new posts by Likers, labeled "People Talking About This"; and reach derived again from the product of those posts times the number of posters' Friends. Likes are also traced to their source, such as Facebook pages, off-Facebook recommendations, ads and so on. Finally, there is the virality factor, the percentage of unique users within reach of your post reacting with posts of their own. This is typically a very tiny number.

Researchers at the Australian marketing think tank Ehrenberg-Bass Institute isolated the People Talking About This results for the two hundred most Liked companies on Facebook over a six-week period in late 2011 relative to the number of Likes and found that only .51 percent of Likers actually posted any brand-related content of any kind, including so much as a single comment. Even so-called high-interest brands, such as Harley-Davidson, Ford Mustang, Louis Vuitton, Chanel and Jack Daniels all registered below 1 percent.[10] Not eye-popping statistics—but ones that get right back to the basics of human behavior. Facebook is fundamentally a social mechanism; it is not a bazaar.

"People don't go to Facebook to look at advertising," says Jeffrey Rohrs. "They go to Facebook to connect with their friends and family, to let people that they might have gotten out of touch with find a way of connecting and reconnecting with them. And keeping folks updated about their lives, very personal things. And that's where the soul of Facebook lies." Yes, for some users, some brand relationships rise to the level of intimacy worthy of ongoing Facebook sharing. Most do not, and to overstep your level is to kill the relationship. Remember the scene in *Swingers*. The schleppy Jon Favreau character had somehow gotten a phone number from a girl he met in a bar, and—in a hilarious but excruciating-to-watch series of late-night answering-machine messages—he tries too soon and too hard to secure a date and in the process so freaks her out she warns him never to call again. Ever. Excessive Facebook familiarity can earn a brand the same treatment.

Trailing Indicator?

And, look, as long as we're accentuating the negative, we may as well throw in what novelist Jonathan Franzen had to say about the Like button, in a commencement speech to 2011 graduates of Kenyon College in Gambier, Ohio. The speech was titled "Liking Is for Cowards":

> If you consider this in human terms, and you imagine a person defined by a desperation to be liked, what do you see? You see a person without integrity, without a center. In more pathological cases, you see a narcissist—a person who can't tolerate the tarnishing of his or her self-image that not being liked represents, and who therefore either withdraws from human contact or goes to extreme, integrity-sacrificing lengths to be likable.[11]

Yow. Franzen is harsh, but he identifies something significant: the temptation to drift from a Relationship Era purposeful sense of self to a manufactured Consumer Era image contrived for maximum likability. For such reasons and others, tech venture capitalist Fred Wilson of Union Square Ventures has blogged his skepticism about investing too much significance in accumulated Likes, which he believes say something about past popularity but foretell little about the future—a classic "trailing indicator," he says. Yet still the raw number of Likes is constantly cited by brands and third parties as evidence of relationship building. Hulu, the online video bundler, gauged the success of Super Bowl ads solely by tabulating Facebook Likes. In the Brazilian stores of fashion retailers, the to-the-second total of C&A's Likes are updated in digital readouts *on every clothes hanger*. And the Croatian file-sharing service Maxxo was one of thousands of companies to issue a press release in 2011 crowing about its surging momentum based on mounting Likes—in this case thirty-five hundred generated through a contest with a cash prize. (A year later the Like population had skyrocketed to four thousand.)

We can't be too haughty about this. You may recall in our chapter on Secret's "Mean Stinks" initiative, we also used Like traffic as a metric of success. Because, at the moment, it's all we've got.

"Likes means 'Oh my God, there's somebody actually out there interacting with me!" says our friend Katie Paine, of the New Hampshire marketing and research consultancy KDPaine & Partners, specialists in public relations and social media measurement. The problem is, she says, once the initial rush of feeling popular fades, brand stewards want to know exactly how popular they are and what that popularity is worth. "What's happening now is that the traditional advertising dollars are being shifted to social media and digital media. And therefore, the traditional advertising people who control those dollars are trying to fit social media into a framework that they can understand. So they want reach and frequency. They want to know the value of a Like—you know, a buck, $3.50. It doesn't work that way. Because what you're dealing with is the absolute fickleness of consumers. 'I like you one day, I may not like you the next.' It's not like you won my trust and my loyalty. . . . Advertisers throw up their hands because they just can't get their heads around it."

What is required, she says, is an effort by the likes of Coca-Cola and Procter & Gamble to do the ROI economics they have so mastered with traditional media advertising, somehow viewing all marketing channels holistically while simultaneously isolating for social, including the computation of true costs. It's a tall order—primarily because the effects of social tend to be lost in a vast sea of ad spending. In October 2012, a year-long effort by eleven industry associations and eight corporations finally yielded a first step: proposed standards for transparency in sourcing and measurement of both engagement levels and conversation.

"We're gonna go through a lot of pain about people ranting about how you can't measure social media, and other people saying you can, and people saying that, well, this is what reach and frequency is in this environment and other people saying no. I mean, I'm part of five committees, I think, trying to set standards for social media measurement and all of that standard stuff is being driven by the need on the part of the advertisers to put real numbers around this thing called social media, this thing called a Like."

Stupid Human Trick

All of this uncertainty may seem dispiriting, exasperating, even infuriating for a marketer who is loath to commit resources to such an unknown. We look at the matter entirely differently, however. We first of all don't obsess about some valuation of the Like, because we know whatever that sum is—exactly as Coca-Cola concludes—it is far greater than the value of a paid-media impression. Andy Sernovitz, CEO of SocialMedia.org, looks at Coca-Cola's "Happiness Machine" viral and defies anybody to compare it to advertising.

"Look," he says, "four million voluntary views where someone said, 'You've got to see this!' are not the same as four million TV impressions. It's a whole different league of that 'engagement' word the ad industry embraced then forgot." Sernovitz also has an ongoing love affair with the public's ongoing love affair with Oreo cookies.

"Go to facebook.com/oreo," he says. "There are 25 million people who want to engage with Oreo. Not because they've seen an Oreo commercial on TV, but because they like Oreos." At the particular moment he was offering this example, the first Oreo-page wall item was a fan photo from a young guy showing how he can place an Oreo on his forehead and—look Ma, no hands!—let it tumble into his mouth. After 24 hours, that Stupid Human Trick had been Liked 685 times. Elsewhere on the page, Nabisco posed a question: "Have you shared an Oreo with anyone lately?" As Sernovitz checked in, he did some calculating: "So far, 946 Like it and 248 people wrote a comment. This is deep. Run the math: the average Facebook person has 150 Friends at this point. I believe that's 180,000 impressions—real impressions, with 10 minutes work, × 365. That's 65 million impressions a year with a personal endorsement of a real person on each and every one.

"Here's an Oreo pound cake recipe: 10,000 Likes, 479 comments, 947 shares. So if you run the math on that, that day they got 1.7 million impressions. For free."

And, to reiterate, each impression arrived with the express endorsement of a friend, or at least a Friend. An ad is someone passing you on the street, someone you may or may not even notice. A Like is an encounter. Maybe it's a kiss and a hug and a catch-up, or maybe it's just a mutual smile in passing, but it is an actual engagement involving at least a modicum of attention and emotion and presumption of ongoingness. A relationship, in other words.

Indeed, relationships have to begin somewhere. They can begin with a transaction or an inquiry. They can begin with a coupon or some other kind of promotion. They can begin outside of the retail realm altogether, as we have seen, between corporations and other stakeholders: employees, neighbors, vendors, shareholders, regulators, legislators or what have you. There is no doubt, however, that a vast and growing number of them begin with the simple click of a pretend button. It is better to light a single candle than curse the darkness, and it is better to embrace the manifest impact of Like rather than curse the absence of ROI metrics. You can't measure love, or faith, or courage, either. Shall we devalue them, as well?

Of course not. Meantime, consider the advice offered by Facebook exec Jesse Dwyer. Rather than falling into the (Consumer Era) trap of trying to convert Likes into transactions, he says, dedicate yourself wholly to turning transactions into Likes.

8

THE SHIFT

The truth will set you free, but first it will piss you off.

—GLORIA STEINEM

We like to call the journey from the Consumer Era to the Relationship Era the Shift. It's a single term that represents all of the upheaval described over the past seven chapters: the shift from mass to micro, the shift from top-down to bottom-up and the shift from traditional marketing to purposeful marketing. That rumbling sound you hear is not just the shifting tectonic plates making sand of what you thought was bedrock. It's also your stomach, viscerally reacting to the stress of adaptation.

And no wonder, because while the geology imagery is useful, another frightening analogy has become the business world's most common means of expressing your predicament. Adapting from one internal infrastructure to another, we are so often told, is like changing the plane's engine in midair. How do you retrofit your institution without bringing ongoing operations—and quarterly growth—crashing to the ground?

Vivid metaphor! Except that it's terrible—because you can't switch out engines in midair, can you? But there are surely ways to make significant changes while still moving forward. Never mind airplanes; there is yet a third analogy that serves best. Think of the baton exchange in a relay race, a carefully calibrated passing, from one body in motion to another, resulting in very little loss of speed or energy and certainly no nosedive to oblivion. There is, of course, an optimal way to time and execute that handoff, to maximize the momentum and minimize lost time. In this chapter we shall explain how to do just that. Till now, most of what we have discussed has been either conceptual or anecdotal. Here we are digging into the process—a process we have divided into two parts.

Introspection

Secret. Panera. Patagonia. Schwab. Krispy Kreme. Method. Louisville Slugger. Zappos. We've offered many a shining example of purpose-driven marketing, and if you've gotten this far you are presumably interested in how to isolate that brand purpose—the idea that inspires what you do and informs every action you take by getting to the core of why you do it. This is not achieved via sensitivity training or New Age crystals or a séance; it's more like making vanilla extract: distillation to the point of essence. Perhaps unsurprisingly, the process is very simple, and very hard.

The process begins with assembling the team and posing one central question: Why does the brand exist? Everybody then contributes thoughts of what they consider to be core beliefs—such as those listed by Charles Schwab when he returned to repair his broken company. This back-and-forth will yield many, many true statements, yet most of those will not address the fundamental question. Some will seem very close to getting at the heart of the matter, but eventually be recognized as merely describing a goal ("to lead the world in microprocessing"), a market condition ("because some people's breath is rank") or simply an irrelevant bit of emotion ("to honor the vision of our sainted founder"). In going through this exercise, it's helpful also to ponder a parallel question: If this brand disappeared from the face of the earth tomorrow, would anybody but financially interested parties care? Look once again at a few purpose statements:

"Secret exists to help women of all ages be fearless."

"Louisville Slugger exists to make players great."

"MEplusYOU exists to advance relationships."

What do all these statements have in common? They are not slogans.

A purpose statement must be derived, not contrived, even if the process seems New Agey, or simplistic or silly. Worry not about *reductio ad absurdum*. What is absurd is the idea that your complex understanding of yesterday's reality will be relevant to a radically different tomorrow. Anyway, simplicity has its merits. To John Mackey, CEO of Whole Foods and proponent of Conscious Capitalism, in the end everything worthwhile is reduced to three Platonic pillars: the good, the true and the beautiful, and a fourth he throws in for good measure, the heroic. If you are honest in your deliberations, this core purpose will be at the heart of everything you do, from your marketing to your hiring to your supply chain to your voice mail greeting. It is *reductio ad lucem:* reduction to enlightenment. A good way to avoid contrivance, by the way, is to avoid hiring some outside agency to "create" your purpose. A skilled facilitator can help you uncover the purpose through painstaking brand archeology, but the purpose is there, and has been there since the beginning. A purpose is not a commodity, and you cannot outsource soul searching. Take this seriously. Your future hinges on it.

For one MEplusYOU client we shall not name, the process of teasing out its purpose lasted seven hours. The entire time the room had been crackling with ideas, insights, challenges, beliefs and passions. When, finally, the clear, succinct statement of purpose was projected onto the conference-room screen, the CMO declared,

"That's it! That's what the brand stands for." Huzzahs and high-fives all around.

Except for one person. The head of marketing communications frowned. Fidgeted. Scowled. "Well, it's what we stand for," she said, "but we can't use it like that. At least two of our competitors could say the same thing. And, for that matter, a few other companies, also. It's just not unique. Couldn't we say. . . ." And thereupon she commenced spouting taglines about how their products were the best, were the coolest, make you rich and beautiful and ward off all disease. It was quintessential Consumer Era thinking: differentiate above all else. What she failed to understand, after a daylong exercise, was that purpose is not positioning. It is not a differentiator contrived to set a brand apart. It is emphatically not a slogan coined to impress outsiders. It is an internal watchword meant to be a point of departure for every aspect of the enterprise.

When MEplusYOU began developing the purpose discovery process a decade ago, it was limited to finding that "why" via the core beliefs flowing into it. Later, though, the process took on more dimensions. Drawing from the writings of author and leadership consultant Simon Sinek, the agency added two more steps to purpose discovery: the "how" and the "what."

"How" a brand expresses its purpose is a codification of how the brand will take a stand in the marketplace. "What" the company does is, well, what the company does—a description of its products and/or services. What's most useful about the exercise, which otherwise might seem idiotic, is the rigor of limiting the descriptions to only what is unimpeachably true. This statement is not for consumers or the trade, and as such served in no way by gloss or puffery. In other words: a built-in reality check.

Recall IKEA's purpose statement: "To create a better everyday life for the many." That's the "why," and it would be hard to argue with either the sentiment or the results. The associated "how" will surely also ring true: "By offering a wide range of well-designed, functional home furnishing products at prices so low that as many people as possible will be able to afford them." And the "what" is

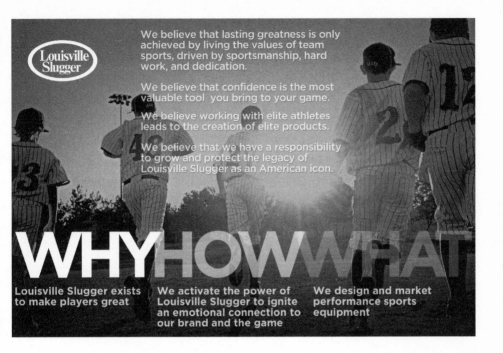

We believe that lasting greatness is only achieved by living the values of team sports, driven by sportsmanship, hard work, and dedication.

We believe that confidence is the most valuable tool you bring to your game.

We believe working with elite athletes leads to the creation of elite products.

We believe that we have a responsibility to grow and protect the legacy of Louisville Slugger as an American icon.

WHY — Louisville Slugger exists to make players great

HOW — We activate the power of Louisville Slugger to ignite an emotional connection to our brand and the game

WHAT — We design and market performance sports equipment

arrayed along the famous IKEA maze-in-a-box: "The IKEA product range focuses on good design and function at a low price. It offers home furnishing solutions for every room in the home. It has something for the romantic at heart, the minimalist and everyone in between. It is coordinated so that no matter which style you prefer, our designers and product developers work hard to ensure that our products meet your day-to-day needs and eliminate the unnecessary."

So let's look at some MEplusYOU clientele, such as Louisville Slugger. The brand may exist to make players great, which is—as the cliché goes—"in its DNA." But how? "We activate the power of Louisville Slugger to ignite an emotional connection to our brand and the game." The what, of course, is manifest, but notably devoid of embellishment: "We design and market performance sports equipment."

Secret is about fearlessness. How: "Secret helps women remain self-assured and confident in all social situations." What: "Secret provides quality underarm deodorant for women."

And MEplusYOU's how: "We apply our Marketing With Purpose formula to achieve superior and sustainable brand results." What: "We provide strategic and creative marketing services."

As we have said, purpose is a point of departure for all of the company's activities, marketing being only one of them. Purpose, though, is not itself a marketing concept. That must be further derived by formulating a Brand Stand, which has a lot in common with positioning but is emphatically not the same thing. We have previously asserted that the positioning impulse leads to inauthenticity and worse, driven as it is by the desire to differentiate from other brands in what may be a parity market. Positioning also operates not from within but based on perceptions of the audience's inclination to buy in. Undeniably, however, the genius of Jack Trout in conceiving the idea back in 1969, is that positioning allows a brand to occupy a unique place in the consumer's psyche. Well, we're fine with that as far as it goes. We offer, however, a more evolved means of occupying the public consciousness. The term *Brand Stand* was coined by Joey Reiman, CEO of BrightHouse in Atlanta, and we are at a loss to improve upon it. A Brand Stand synthesizes the intrinsic attributes of the good or service with its emotional appeal (if any) and with the values it shares with stakeholders. It is an expression of the Three Cs: credibility, care and congruence. Or, if you like, it is the totality of the why/how/what trinity of the purpose proposition.

Once again, this is not a slogan or a selling proposition; it is a point of view. If purpose is the internal understanding of why the brand exists, Brand Stand is the internal shorthand for how the brand faces the outside world. You could argue, for instance, that Apple's positioning has always been to be the heroic alternative for independent thinkers—that is, the anti-PC. We would say equally it has always stood for something rooted deep within its identity: technological and design elegance.

Purpose represents the brand's inner self. Brand Stand is the sum of its outward projection. Remember, this is no longer the Consumer Era. You don't dictate an image; you own a point of view. How the public processes this can be influenced on the margins by advertising, more so by your explicit and implicit promises, more still by your outreach activities with your audiences, but ultimately by the totality of what you project. Not to belabor the point, your success or failure will reside in the accumulation of your relationships. Next we will explore the process of creating them.

How to Venn Friends and Influence People

To reiterate, this book does not intend to be a tutorial on social marketing. Relationship Era principles apply across the board to all channels of connection between brands and human beings. For the sake of clarity, however, in mapping the processes of Relationship Era marketing we shall isolate on the social sphere. This will yield a six-point checklist that applies, plus or minus, across all channels. It represents, as it were, the relay racer accepting the baton. But first: a quick journey to the wonderful world of Venn diagrams.

You most likely did these in sixth-grade math class, or thereabouts, as teachers attempted to visually reinforce their lessons on set theory. A Venn diagram consists of a series of circles, each containing the entire population of its set. The degree of intersection reflects commonalities in the circles' populations. The set of all dogs, for example, would not intersect at all with the set representing members of Congress, because dogs cannot vote, fund-raise or pander.

The set of *Star Trek* nerds and the set of those who have adjusted poorly to the challenges of life have a significant intersection. The darkened area where the circles overlap represents losers who are also *Star Trek* buffs.

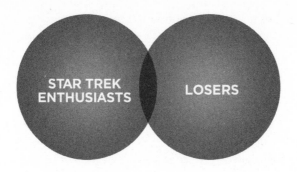

Often multiple sets have multiple intersections, but in varying degrees. The population of all people known by all three of their names includes significant chunks of both the musician population (John Lee Hooker, Stevie Ray Vaughan, John Cougar Mellencamp, Billy Ray Cyrus, Olivia Newton John, David Lee Roth, Mary Chapin Carpenter and Jerry Lee Lewis) and also the assassin population (James Earl Ray, Mark David Chapman, Lee Harvey Oswald, John Wilkes Booth, Sara Jane Moore and Jared Lee Loughner). There is only a negligible crossover between musicians and assassins, attributable mainly to John Wilkes Booth's prowess with the jaw's harp.

Yes, for expressing the common population of sets, you can't beat a Venn diagram. Nor can you beat it for visualizing Relationship Era marketing.

Imagine that you manufacture a certain product: a fancy kitchen sponge called NeetFreek, no more absorbent than others but manufactured entirely with recycled shopping bags and treated to kill surface bacteria on contact. Like any manufacturer, it behooves you to do right by your various stakeholders: employees, neighbors, shareholders, vendors, distributors, regulators, governments, retailers and consumers. But for the moment, let's pay specific attention to present and potential retail purchasers. Most likely the brand is awash in segmentation studies slicing and dicing consumer behavior by demographics, psychographics, media consumption and so on. These are rudimentary tools of Consumer Era marketing, as a preliminary step in determining what message to fashion to momentarily grab their attention, and where to deliver it. In the Relationship Era, the approach is very close to the opposite. Now you must first determine your own essence, which will be projected not just by your product but by all you do. Your purpose, your values, your interests and your conduct will create a sort of aura that will variously overlap with the values and interests of many sets of consumers. Whereupon—in the Consumer Era—you would immediately pounce on them with advertising. In the Relationship Era, locating the common ground is also the beginning—but not of a campaign. It is the beginning of a conversation.

Let's say your brand's purpose was "NeetFreek exists to make cleaning cleaner." Its Brand Stand, like everything else at Freek-Corp., is informed by that purpose, but it's a big world out there and not everyone is motivated by what motivates a sponge manufacturer. Hence NeetFreek's Brand Stand: "We're gonna make it easier for you, and fun and kind of inspiring to do the best you can."

Having codified its point of view, the brand must now make sure its products or services meet the promise, that its personality invites others to collaborate based on shared interests and values, however profound or mundane. For a brand like NeetFreek, there could be many such overlaps.

Those darkened, oblong shapes of intersection are where it all takes place. But how to know where the overlaps are? They obviously cannot be identified by jawboning in a conference room. To

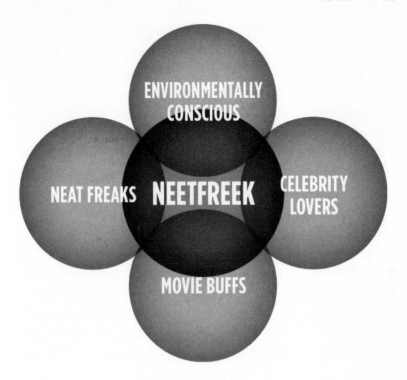

understand what a brand shares with its audiences, it had better know exactly what those audiences have to say.

Step 1. Listen.

After all, is listening not the best way to cultivate any fledgling relationship? It is, first of all, considerate and unselfish. It is flattering to the speaker. It is data rich. What better way to learn about the person than by paying close attention to her stated thoughts, desires, interests, peeves, experiences and so on? Furthermore, it is difficult, while listening in silence, to make an ass of yourself. What is different, and advantageous, for brands is the capacity to monitor hundreds of millions of voices at the same time, to sift like the National Security Agency through all sorts of public chatter to discover who is saying what about what or whom at any moment in time or over any period of time. Through free applications like Twitter Search or Google Blog Search, any brand can gather more raw material about its place—or its competitors' place—in the conversation than ever imaginable. Many private vendors offer sophisticated analytics, including sentiment analysis that divines the trajectory of public opinion about your company and brand. Monitoring this traffic is the bare minimum for any brand, company, organization, institution or individual.

You find out where you stand in the public's mind across all areas of your activities.

You can quickly address individual customer issues—or other stakeholder issues—on a one-to-one basis. This offers specific information as to possible internal problems, silences squeaky wheels and in turn creates opportunities for positive word of mouth.

You can learn more than market research has ever told you about the interests, values, likes, dislikes, passions and fears of those in your sphere.

You get early warning of opportunities, or trouble, ahead.

You can have your assumptions about how your audiences think and behave turned upside down.

Consider World Vision USA. World Vision is a nonprofit that funds humanitarian work in the poorest nations by offering "sponsorships" of children. There are several such organizations; this one has nothing to do with Sally Struthers or Save the Children. Indeed, unlike others with an advertising-purchased higher profile, World Vision is famously efficient. Whereas some nonprofits are not far removed from Ponzi schemes, generating donations to pay for the cost of generating donations, World Vision spends only 14 percent of revenue on administration and fund-raising.[1] As an explicitly Christian ministry, it is also very clear on its purpose: "to serve alongside the poor and oppressed as a demonstration of God's unconditional love for all people."[2]

Before the process began, the creative team knew only one thing for sure: Whatever forms of engagement might ultimately emerge, nothing would be icky. They would not prey the guilt of the fortunate in the name of the unfortunate.

That notion didn't last long. The online chatter quickly yielded a big surprise: Nobody in the social sphere was complaining about being made by charities to feel guilty. On the contrary, feelings of being the disproportionate beneficiary of affluence—that is, counting your blessings—seemed to undergird very positive feelings about self-sacrifice. Remember, the essence of Relationship Era marketing is to find shared values and shared value for seller and buyer alike. In this case, the money for good works might serve both the charity and the psychic and emotional needs of the givers. The more the team thought, the more they wondered: Without guilt, would we have the same degree of empathy, the same sense of responsibility or even a moral compass to guide us? A new consensus quickly formed. To paraphrase Gordon Gekko: Guilt is good. So instead of arbitrarily dismissing an authentically human emotion, the team contrived to cultivate it.

"Our ministry to the poor may look like a water project or an economic project," says Scott Chin, e-business executive director at World Vision USA, "but our donors, too, have a need. They have a need to engage in philanthropy. We provide an avenue and an opportunity to engage in tackling poverty."

One lesson from that episode is that true Relationship Era marketing leaves all parties feeling good about the transaction. A second lesson is that if you are a charity—or if you are anything else—heed Mr. Rogers and Polonius. Be true to yourself; the Relationship Era is no place for posturing. A third moral of the story is the immense value in simply listening—and not merely to the people talking about you. That would be so un-Venn. Once again, there's a whole world out there.

Let's go back to NeetFreek sponges. Recall the Venn diagram of four separate overlapping areas of interest: the environmentally conscious, neat freaks, movie buffs and celebrity lovers. Knowing that these (and other categories) represent substantial areas of aligned interests, you must also carefully track the chatter in those communities, to understand their preoccupations, values, likes, dislikes, passions and fears. Your goal is, after all, to find common ground and cultivate it. You'd best survey their acreage.

But, for heaven's sake, this is a search for affinities, not for prospects. If you tune in to, say, pet-lover chatter and find no common ground, so be it. Remember Matt Dillon's character in *There's Something About Mary*? He eavesdropped on Mary (Cameron Diaz) and discovered she was interested in architecture, Nepal and working with mentally challenged kids—so he pretended to be an architect just back from Nepal and on his way to a volunteer gig with, as he put it, "retards." He was, of course, eventually exposed as a fraud and humiliated. So, yeah, don't do that.

Step 2. Define social personality.

By now the point has been made many times: Relating as a brand is fundamentally the same as relating as a person. There is, however, one problem with that fundamental truth. Brands are not single people. And not only are brands not individuals, even the brand's online persona will not be expressed by one individual. There may be a half dozen, or even in some cases hundreds, of employees with responsibility for representing the brand's thoughts, observations, questions, interests, boasts, excuses, apologies and attitudes on Facebook, Twitter and so on. And if they all try to channel the brand as they personally experience it, in all probability they will present as many different faces to the public as they have employees. For Zappos, such individuality is part of the corporate culture, maybe even the defining part of the culture. Most companies, however, will benefit from a little more uniformity in what persona its brands wish to project.

Obviously, that persona should be an authentic representation of all the purpose and values we've discussed till now, but that still leaves plenty of room for wild swings in subject matter, language, tone, style and, well, personality. As such, unless you go the Zappos route, all involved must embrace a set of consistent characteristics personifying the brand. This requires imagining the ideal human frontline representative and listing his or her personality traits— much as you'd list them in psychographic segmentation.

Meghan, the imaginary spokes-Twitterer for NeetFreek is bubbly with lots of self-awareness and room for self-deprecation. She is herself a neat freak, and an eco-do-gooder, but she can make fun of her fixations and also of her tendency to rush up to anyone vaguely famous to get a camera phone snapshot. She's quite knowledgeable about polymers, but no scientist; she has a thing for capri pants and flats, because that's what smart moms always wear in the household-cleaners ads. She loves Clay Aiken and Julia Roberts and makes no apologies for that. She found out Howard Hughes was a truly pathological neat freak and has learned every weird detail of his life. And, most of all, she is the virtual embodiment of your brand's core purpose. Yes, a brand needs a social voice, but a brand is not defined by its social voice. D. H. Lawrence put it nicely:

> I want relations which are not purely personal, based on purely personal qualities; but relations based upon some unanimous accord in truth or belief, and a harmony of purpose, rather than of personality.[3]

All the more reason to make clear: we are certainly not proposing that NeetFreek employees pose as a fictional character. Nor are we suggesting that a brand assume some fantasy persona, like an avatar in *Second Life*. We simply wish for front-line employees to consider, "If a real-life Meghan were asked to represent the accumulated *actual interests and values* of the NeetFreek brand, where would she be coming from?" Then the team can channel her motivations and mannerisms as a proxy for the entire brand.

On that point though, here is another absolute "don't": Do not let Meghan sound like some sort of lifeless p.r. bot. Companies are so terrified of empowering junior employees with Twitter autonomy they tend to restrict them to certain templates and even scripts, much as they do with their tele-reps. As a result, an opportunity for human contact is obliterated by stilted language. In fact, exactly the same phenomenon takes place when *senior* employees speak in public; every word goes through a p.r. wringer until the life has been squeezed out of it. So here's an exercise:

Talk to your cousin. Give him or her a call. Talk about your business, your brand, your successes, your failures, your plans, your challenges, your intractable problems. Take note of how you frame these things and of how you phrase them—and to the responses you get, for, after all, this is a conversation. Good. Now go back and look at your external marketing materials, your press releases, your annual report. Perhaps you'll notice a slight difference in language, tone, clarity, candor and style. Exactly who do you think your customers are that you need to communicate with them as if they had no blood coursing through their veins? They are warm-blooded people, cousins one and all. So try speaking with them as if they were, and listen to what they have to say. And make sure all your Meghans do the same.

Exactly who do you think your customers are
that you need to communicate with them as if
they had no blood coursing through their veins?

Step 3. Join the conversation.

Relationship Era thinking is not confined to e-relationships. In the end, we are all flesh and blood and this is not some elaborate SIM game we're describing; it is a way of business life. By the same token, however, as a percentage of the total universe of interactions, online is increasingly where the rubber meets the road. So now what?

You have meditated and settled on purpose. You have determined to create and nurture relationships. You have listened diligently to the exterior monologues of stakeholders across the board. You have drafted guidance to your people to maximize the cohesiveness of your online persona. At this point you are probably itching to get out there in the social space like Secret and foment one or more revolutionary movements around your brand.

Right. Not so fast. Imagine a dinner party. You and the spouse have been invited to join a group of friends whose kids go to the same school, and who have formed significant bonds around soccer, classroom activities, birthdays, sleepovers and so on. You are the outlier. You got to know Kyla from Pilates, where you two cut up every week while working futilely together against nature and gravity. But at the party at the first opportunity, you—the relative stranger in the group—turn the conversation toward Pilates and keep it there . . . to the diminishing interest and growing embarrassment of the dinner company, including your husband, who keeps glaring at you. In effect, through sheer force of will, you have hijacked the conversation and made everybody uncomfortable, except for the ones who comfortably decide you are an obnoxious intruder. This is obviously not a great way to start with near-total strangers. At that stage, you might as well get sloppy on the white wine, because you've already lost this crowd.

The dynamics are no different in social media. Therefore, enter the conversation not by calling attention to yourself with offers and promotion and fledgling schemes. First, simply share. Pass along items of interest to your Venn groups that may be interested in them. You have the wherewithal to rigorously scour the Internet for content; why keep the goodies to yourself? Share relevant news, information, videos, charts, quotations and other content—including just the highly cool and very fun—with potentially interested parties. *Do not—repeat, do not—attempt to gild the lily with some sort of brand spin.* At least, not yet.

"In general," says marketing professor Jonah Berger of the Wharton School of Business, "we found a negative relationship between brandedness and sharing." He and fellow researchers concluded this in a combination of laboratory experiments and auditing of YouTube video pass-along. And why should this be so? Because branded content looks like an ad, and (we repeat) to the public all ads are spam. According to Visible Measures, the video analytics and online ad platform—*a company in the viral-video business*—six of seven videos, even with the help of big media buys, fail to reach one million views. That means achieving less reach than one spot on Anderson Cooper's CNN show one time. However, if you gain credibility as a trusted curator, you will be taken more seriously when—and if—you presume to lead. There may well come a time to create content, and the rewards can be plentiful. Just not quite yet. In the interim, confine your participation to being the best forwarder *ever*, and, naturally, to directly addressing complaints or questions posed to you or about you online. How do you build personal relationships? As a rule, a fleeting encounter does not lead immediately to marriage and joint ownership of assets, or to deep and abiding friendship including gift exchanges and golfing trips and late-night phone-call privileges. It might lead to a coffee, though, or a lunch, or a ball game. Or to a glimmer of recognition and some friendly but awkward conversation, because nobody remembers the other's name. All of which is more intimate than your relationship with, say, Geico insurance—no matter how many billions of media dollars they've invested in the gecko—because you are strangers.

Ordinary social relations are not just a useful analogy to business in the Relationship Era; they are a near absolute template. Let us consider briefly that question of what level of permission is conferred on a brand when somebody clicks Like. In the previous chapter, you saw that 15 percent of Facebook users are practically ready to surrender their debit card PIN numbers, but 39 percent think a Like-ing permits nothing at all. To them it means, "Yeah, nice stuff, but don't call me; I'll call you."

Imagine a situation from actual, analog life. You are at back-to-school night for your fifth grader, your butt squeezed into a tiny classroom chair and the vice principal comes into the room to brief the parents on the school's zero-tolerance policy for tween violence. Here she comes, Dr. Filkins, and she looks exactly like Angelina Jolie and you and another dad exchange a quick surreptitious glance, eyes widened and just the barest hint of a smile crossing your lips. Later, while waiting to tell the teacher about your kids' peanut allergies, you shake hands with the other dad and exchange pleasantries. Here's what's permissible: a vague promise to meet again at the PTA meeting, or to set up playdates for the children, either of which could lead to an ongoing relationship and perhaps someday even friendship.

Here's what's not permissible: "Nice to meet you, Bill. I'm Doug Levy. In the trunk of my car I have one hundred copies of my new book, *Can't Buy Me Like*. Wanna buy one?"

Bill would be some combination of put off, embarrassed and offended. He would make sure to avoid this Levy guy at the PTA meeting. And there is a high probability he'd tell other dads that Doug Levy is a total dick. So why would anyone behave differently in the name of their brand? Useful advice in business and in life: Don't be a dick.

Useful advice in business and in life:
Don't be a dick.

We are speaking, after all, about human nature. Once you internalize the notion that human emotions and behavior do not significantly change when it's time to go shopping, and that we increasingly are judging businesses in human terms, and that strong relationships last a lifetime, it's easy to see why interacting with the public through digital channels conforms entirely to the standards of flesh-and-blood fellowship. Here's one way of looking at how the mentality of the Consumer Era fails in the Relationship Era:

Social Strategy

CONSUMER ERA	RELATIONSHIP ERA
Objective: Acquisition	**Objective:** Engagement
Strategy: Go viral	**Strategy:** Give consumers something to talk about
Starts with: Promotion	
Messaging: "Follow Me on _____"	**Starts with:** Listening
Success measure: Number of views/impressions and acquisitions	**Messaging:** From consumer to consumer
	Success measure: Level of content sharing and engagement

Step 4. Lead the conversation.

If you have any kind of brand profile, and if you have been a good social-media participant, at this stage you will have an organically accrued following in various online channels. Now, finally, you are

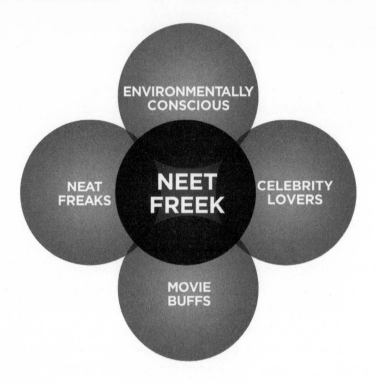

in a position to be proactive. Like a dinner guest who has been part of the flow of conversation, you have earned the attention of the crowd—or crowds—once you decide to assert yourself. Your organization houses great expertise over a wide array of subject matter, your brand as a whole has a point of view, and in your various Venn overlaps you have significant numbers of interested parties prepared to take you seriously. But not by delivering ads or press releases disguised as content. You are still in a human conversation, and the rules of engagement haven't changed. What's changed is the readiness of your publics to pay attention. That is a precious opportunity. Recall NeetFreek.

Because NeetFreek is manufactured using no virgin cellulose but rather 100 percent postconsumer shredded plastic, one of your obvious constituencies would be the environmentally conscious. Now, suppose you were in a room with them. Would you talk a lot about sponging? Would you talk about the depleting ozone layer? Or would you maybe discuss matters that are of direct interest to both parties—that is, your Venn overlaps. Maybe that means you'd be talking about novel ways to turn nonbiodegradable waste into something useful. Plastic bags, automobile tires, motor oil, plastic soda bottles, foam packing peanuts, whatever. In all probability, you'd share stories about projects you'd heard about, or maybe you'd blue-sky about the possibilities. Old ballpoint pens chopped into aggregate for highway concrete? Who knows?

Now, forget the small room and resume your life as the NeetFreek brand. Within that general topic of conversation, there is an unlimited number of ways in which you could carry on an extended conversation with this constituency—in advertising, yes, but also on Facebook, on Twitter, in crowd-sourcing projects, in contests, in sponsorships, in philanthropy. The same goes for your constituency of, well, neat freaks. There is an equally unlimited opportunity to engage them, on an ongoing basis, in the matters of house hygiene: cleaning tips, tales from UnderTheSink, the exchange of funny anecdotes (or horrifying ones), the science of household bacteria, things you can do with your discarded NeetFreeks and so on. There is no need for us to lecture you on coming up with ideas. You pay badly dressed people to do that for you.

No need to stop at one, either, because Facebook is free. In the world of paid media, only a handful of marketers have the resources to tailor discrete campaigns for audiences of different demographic and psychographic characteristics. Most notable among them, perhaps, is Anheuser-Busch, which for decades has been able to target older traditionalists with one set of Budweiser ads, young people with another, blue-collar workers with a third and so on. In the world of social media, every marketer is virtual-Budweiser: free to separately address each of its major and minor segments at negligible additional cost. So NeetFreek, for instance, can have fun with its Venn overlap with moviegoers: "Hey, everybody! What movie scenes can you think of where someone is sponging? Who's the biggest star with a sponge?" Maybe this could lead to an advocacy campaign, like the one from the antismoking lobby, beseeching Hollywood to use only environmentally friendly products in its scrubbing scenes. (Except for criminals cleaning up blood. They can use Formula 409 and Brawny.) As for finding celebrity NeetFreek enthusiasts—explicitly not as paid endorsers but plucked from the real world of eco-consciousness—well, duh.

Perhaps NeetFreek might declare itself as a signatory to a fair-labor-practices pledge. Or maybe it solicits ideas for a Neet Olympics. ("Yo, everybody: What would the events be?") Maybe it asks for the Ten Best Sponging Scenes in Hollywood history. Maybe it makes a movie spoof *Bac(teria) to the Future*—or asks its fans to do so. Maybe it shows video of plastic shopping bags being hauled from recycling centers, washed, shredded and fabricated into sponges. And, meantime, it continues passing along cool stuff and commentary to its Vennsters who might appreciate it, and responding to every "NeetFreek jammed my garbage disposal" tweet that surfaces.

All of the above activities serve three purposes: (1) they accelerate engagement with existing followers, (2) they expand your reach to new followers as the signal radiates outward, and (3) they enhance your credibility as a source across the various Venn communities you are engaging and beyond. At this stage, your brand personality— the Collective Meghan—has been established. When you speak, your followers are hearing a consistent voice they associate with "those folks at NeetFreek." To paraphrase Sally Field, they like you, *they like you.* They may even Like you. Therefore, do not at this stage lapse into corporate speak. Encourage your Meghans to be human.

One of the great social-media blunders came back in 2011, when a lowly employee of Chrysler's social agency, supposedly thinking he was tweeting on his personal rather than corporate account, sent the following message to @ChryslerAutos followers as follows: "*I find it ironic that Detroit is known as the #motorcity yet no one here knows how to fucking drive.*" What happened next was the agency, New Media Strategies, fired the employee. What happened next was Chrysler fired New Media Strategies.[4] Hmm. This was probably the only Chrysler tweet ever tweeted with a semblance of human feeling and believability, and yet it caused a bloodbath. Doubly ironic is the fact that Chrysler had just commenced a raw and gritty multi-hundred-million-dollar advertising campaign affecting the styles and rhythms of the streets and starring Eminem, among the most profane entertainers ever to emerge from Motown. So how did one hilariously honest F-bomb constitute a firing offense?

Here's what the company should have done: (1) apologize in a tweet; (2) start a conversation about where the worst drivers are; (3) start another conversation about similarly embarrassing "open-mic" moments; and (4) give the guy a big, fucking raise.

Step 5. Ignite and invite action.

At last! You are but one step from enlightenment. You have arrived at the fifth level: the stage where the brand has a chance to do something nakedly self-interested, by means of doing something contrived to attract the interest of your followers and to attract more followers overall. Which usually means giving them something. Perhaps a freebie, perhaps a coupon, perhaps (sort of) exclusive access to certain content or to certain merchandise or to a celebrity, perhaps a fun online activity or even a useful application.

It is true that this entire book is premised on being admired for your own intrinsic self. And it is true that gaining playmates by giving them your lunch money creates dubious and fragile ties. It is equally true, though, that people like getting stuff for free. If you stand on the playground tossing coins by the handful, you will draw a crowd. For NeetFreek, the bounty could manifest itself in many ways. Perhaps a "Put Us Out of Business" copromotion with supermarkets, offering a free NeetFreek for shoppers who buy $200 or more in groceries and pack them in their own bags. Or a free download of an Angry Sponges game, or a $100,000 Neatest Mom competition. People do stop to grab when the piñata opens. Sure, some of them will lose interest once the SWAG shower has ended, but others—once you have their attention—might very well stick around and try to get to know you. If your promotion is at all relevant to what you do, your brand may resonate in ways it had not before. Among the greatest examples of activity as giveaway was the famous OfficeMax "Elf Yourself" campaign of 2006. The online tool allowed you to upload your own photo and make it the face of a dancing Christmas elf. Some people thought it would be fun. More than five hundred million uploads later, OfficeMax has not only sold a lot of office supplies to people who came for the elfing but has established itself as a perennial legitimate source for holiday stocking stuffers. Oh, and it has every elfer's e-mail address in its database.

Gaining playmates by giving them your lunch money creates dubious and fragile ties.

Mind you, people do indeed like free gifts, but that is by no means limited to monetary value. There are other rewards. In South Africa, the burger chain Wimpy began by giving a laugh to a mere fifteen people. The occasion was the introduction of Braille menus for the visually handicapped, so the ad agency, Metropolitan Republic, painstakingly baked fifteen hamburger buns on which the sesame seeds spelled out, in Braille, "100% pure beef burger made for you." The burgers were served to folks at three organizations for the blind, where the recipients were so amused they spread the word via Braille newsletter and online channels to eight hundred thousand others in the vision-impaired community.[5] The YouTube video bragging about the stunt earned another five hundred thousand views[6] mainly, of course, in the sighted world, where people have no strict interest in Braille menus but did enjoy watching the smiles on the faces of people reading their lunch.

Vicarious fun is still fun. P&G shot commercials in essentially real time in which Isaiah Mustafa—the insanely popular Old Spice guy—personally addressed individuals who had commented on one of his recent hilarious commercials. Those lucky few were chosen, after some quick research, based on their degree of influence. Sure enough, when the quickie spots were posted, they shot around the Web at warp speed. The videos averaged twenty-three million views.

So, yes, one way of initiating a relationship is by handing out gifts. An even better way is to ask for a favor.

As counterintuitive as this may sound, but a fact long since enshrined in the literature of psychology, is that human beings will identify with those they have been called upon to assist. This is called the Ben Franklin effect, named after the inventor/publisher/ diplomat/lothario/C-note star who first described it. As the story goes, Franklin had a fraught relationship with a rival legislator— basically, the guy refused to even acknowledge him—and this our famously fraternal founding father found frustrating. So, as he related in his autobiography (and cribbed by us from Wikipedia) Franklin forged a plan:

> Having heard that he had in his library a certain very scarce and curious book, I wrote a note to him, expressing my desire of perusing that book, and requesting he would do me the favour of lending it to me for a few days. He sent it immediately, and I return'd it in about a week with another note, expressing strongly my sense of the favour. When we next met in the House, he spoke to me (which he had never done before), and with great civility; and he ever after manifested a readiness to serve me on all occasions, so that we became great friends, and our friendship continued to his death.[7]

What Franklin had exploited was the psychological reaction to cognitive dissonance. His rival felt antipathy toward him, yet being a gentleman, fulfilled Franklin's request. This caused conflicting, or dissonant, emotions for the guy; he had just helped the man he loathed. And so, to reconcile the inner conflict, he had to cease loathing him. No more cognitive dissonance. Lifelong friendship. As such, even brands such as General Electric—if they seek assistance from those who harbor enduring resentment—have a chance, all else being equal, to entirely reframe the terms of the relationship.

"I'm quite convinced it all boils down to minimization of cognitive dissonance," says Adam Ferrier, consumer psychologist and cofounder of the Australian agency Naked Communications.

For the entire Consumer Era, marketers burned ad fuel to persuade, persuade, persuade. Or at least to impress, impress, impress—which, as we asserted earlier, is unsustainable. "Actually changing behavior through rational or emotional persuasion is quite cumbersome and not particularly effective," Ferrier agrees. "And the effect is often very short term. Hence, if you don't keep persuading, people don't keep buying."

On the other hand, seeking help from your various stakeholders obliges them to align their thoughts, feelings and actions along Ben Franklin lines. "Getting them to act is going to be a more effective way to change their attitudes toward their brand, and to change their behavior," Ferrier says. "You can have the relationship start by asking someone to do you a favor and invest something of themselves into you. If they want ownership, give them more ownership. Get them into your brand and your business as much as possible. Let them become co-producers of your brand and they become more loyal."

Of course, as Ferrier astutely observes, "Unilever can't call you and say, 'Mate, would you help me move my flat?'" There are other ways to get positive action from the public. Naked won an Effie with an initiative for Jarrah, which is a brand of flavored instant coffees that was struggling against the category leader Twinings. Everybody in the category sampled like crazy. You couldn't open your mailbox without instant coffee packets tumbling out. So Naked persuaded Jarrah to tell the public no dice. If you want a sample, you have to go to a Web site, fill out a form and choose your own damn flavor. Then, and only then, would they send it to you. They were so inundated with requests they had to discontinue the offer early. Sales went up 11 percent. And stayed there.

Hmm. It's an impressive result, but the underlying psychology also sounds a bit manipulative—in exactly the sort of way that consumers have long thought advertising to be. Is this a case wherein understanding the human response to cognitive dissonance is exploitive, like the barroom pickup artist's trick of getting the women to buy a drink for him? Unsurprisingly, Ferrier says no.

"It's not in anyone's interest to hoodwink the consumer. If you don't return that favor, your newfound relationship isn't going to last very long. Just like any relationship, there has to be reciprocity and a positive and continual value exchange between both parties."

On the subject of P&G, the Secret endeavors on behalf of women ski jumping, Diana Nyad's brave swim and antibullying were themselves a gift to Secret's Venn overlappers. It was the gift of enabling disparate voices to be heard—a principle that also fueled Dell's Ideastorm.com consumer-suggestion Web site and MyStarbucksIdea.com. More than twenty-eight thousand ideas for coffee drinks were submitted, not to mention music and merchandise, atmosphere, social responsibility and tea—each submission representing a stakeholder staking incrementally more ownership of the brand. One direct result: those green thingamabobs at Starbucks that look like they should have cocktail olives speared on them. A fan suggested a stopper to prevent spillage from travel lids, and now these little green sticks are plunged into to-go coffees the world over. At that stage, actually, a brand has ventured beyond mere ignition; it has achieved the sixth level.

Step 6. Inspire greater collaboration.

Or, as we call it, nirvana. This is where your Venn overlaps become extensions of your brand. It is where nominal outsiders become your de facto marketers, p.r. agents, product developers, business consultants and production companies. That is why Secret's "Let Her Jump," Dell's Ideastorm.com and MyStarbucksIdea.com dwell here. In each case, discrete Venn communities collaborated with the brand to achieve results the brand could not have achieved by itself—a process that can span the ridiculous to the sublime. Sometimes it's amateur creatives producing Doritos commercials for the Super Bowl, usually involving some poor wretch getting kicked in his privates. On the other side is the rock artist Beck, who in 2012 released his latest album without recording a single note; he released instead sheet music and asked fans to become makers. It's not just collaboration; it's a role reversal. The audience now performs and the artist listens.

In the corporate realm, the defining example was provided by Lego for its Mindstorms line of robotic toys. Lego convened an ad hoc Mindstorms User's Panel, a group of enthusiasts who spent months at their own expense designing the new product line and thereupon years talking it up in their social circles. Without a penny of paid media behind it, the relaunched Mindstorms line became the most profitable in Lego corporate history. Similarly, Kraft Foods has an ongoing "Innovate with Kraft" program soliciting business ideas not from its ninety thousand employees but from the other eight billion humans who eat. This outreach has spawned, among other things, Kraft Bagel-fuls, which have cream cheese pre*schmear*ed for your convenience.

Now maybe cream cheese convenience doesn't rock your world. What it does do is include the bagel-eating community in developments of interest to bagel eaters and bagel bakers alike. That is a moment of Venn. Likewise the experience of World Vision USA, which ultimately went online asking donors to share personal stories of giving in their own words. Some sponsor out of grief for their own lost child, some out of religious duty, some out of philanthropic spirit, some out of naked guilt—and they all have a tale to tell. The creative platform—"What Moves You?"—was equal parts slogan and solicitation, yielding many inspiring narratives, some wrenching, some plain, all shared in all media and social-media channels. Instead of preaching to the choir, World Vision was letting the choir do the preaching. And in perfect fulfillment of the Relationship Era's emphasis on shared value, the donors revealed themselves to be beneficiaries, as well.

Not a bad example, World Vision. But the truly quintessential case history—one that turned collaboration into something tantalizingly close to a perpetual-motion machine—is among the three or four most successful marketing campaigns of the past fifty years. It was widely admired and studied, yet somehow few have understood the significance of a system hidden in plain view. Weirdly, it has been missed even by the ad agency industry, which is in no way prepared for life after the media commission. The marketer?

Barack Obama.

Relax. This is not in any way, shape or form about politics, policy, ideology or the audacity of hope. Rather, it's about audacity born of hopelessness. There was a time in 2007 when Obama was not a mesmerizing-nigh-unto-messianic world figure, but merely a skinny rookie U.S. senator who made 'em swoon on the stump but had a low national profile and a whole lot less money than Democratic front-runner Senator Hillary Clinton. What he did have, though, was his intrinsic qualities as a candidate and a core of supporters for whom the word *activist* scarcely conveyed their devotion. They were more like cultists, or Nordstrom customers. And with every victory, campaign strategists understood, the core would grow, donate more money, raise more money, spread the word and everything else an insurgent candidacy needs. As such, to build momentum, the Obama campaign blew most of its bankroll on the Iowa caucuses. His stunning victory there validated the strategy. But then they were faced with Super Tuesday, including the California primary, when hundreds of delegates would be up for grabs. Coming out of Iowa, they had momentum, but Clinton had $40 million. And getting creamed in California would have meant a loss of momentum, and everything that a presidential campaign loses along with it.

Enter two California staffers, Jeff Coleman and Brent Messenger, young tech guys charged with harnessing the knowledge and expertise of volunteers from the likes of Yahoo and Google, in order to harness the enthusiasm of seventy thousand like-minded just plain folks.

"We put together a team of developers and built software to manage a very structured network of volunteer activists," says Coleman. "The idea was to get the right information out to the right people and have them report back to us.

"Another way to put it is that in Iowa there are 100,000 votes. For those 100,000 votes, we had something on the order of 400–500 field organizers. In California, we were trying to get just shy of 5 million votes, and we had six people. We tried to use software to replace those organizers."

Tried and mammothly succeeded. By empowering volunteers with software that sliced and diced registered Democrats every which way, the volunteers were able not merely to canvass but to engage in actual conversations with exactly the people predisposed to have them. This enabled Obama to exponentially increase not just his reach but his engagement. In turning customers into salespeople, Obama amassed more than 5 million Facebook friends, 13 million e-mail subscribers, 3 million online donations and an average 8.5 million visits to My-BarackObama.com every month leading up to election day. While Clinton was outspending him 30 to 1, he was outfriending her by 1,000 to 1. For her $30 million she won 204 delegates. For his $1 million, Obama won 166.[8]

From that point, the campaign took the software and the strategy to every subsequent primary state. By that time, too, cash money was rolling in—thanks to the very human assistance that had been so inexpensive—and Obama all but ran the table to the nomination. And the presidency.

What makes these activities nirvana is that they represent the most intimate relationships achievable among nominal strangers in the form of extraordinary identification with the brand. You are a part of them and they become part of you. They are not Friends. They are friends.

Measure.

We can't call this Step 7, because that would imply "last." In fact, it is something that should be done at the outset and constantly, because online the very process of listening yields the tools for measuring the ebb and flow of your social presence. Whether with Google analytics, or Twitter search or socialmention.com, or any of the commercially available research tools, a brand is able to gauge its social impact in real time. Are there particular posts or topics that resonate especially with your publics? Are there topics that land with a sickening thud? Have you done or said something that actually drives people away? (Oh, it happens. See Chapter 11, This Could Be the End of a Previously Very Good Relationship.) The negligible cost in time and money permit a nearly infinite opportunity for A/B testing, along traditional direct-marketing lines. With the caveat that every outward signal be informed by brand purpose, not just by what gets the most attention, it's easy to optimize outreach as you go. It is also easy to track the competition along all the same criteria.

Critically important as it is, the process of measurement can be dispiriting, for reliable ROI metrics are elusive and the marketer is forced to reckon at all times with numbers that seem preposterously small compared with the bounty of advertising reach. In that sense, the shift from the Consumer Era to the Relationship Era is like going from the vast corn and wheat fields of the Midwest to a little truck farm in western Maryland. Equally dispiriting is the labor of tending to the truck farm; so much digging and hoeing and weeding and watering for such a tiny yield. Be not tempted, however, to impose a Consumer Era mentality on these efforts. At a conference we attended in July 2012, a manager of global customer relations management and social for Amway spoke eloquently about the value of ongoing dialogue to a direct-selling organization—but then he explained how Amway maximizes the value: by grading consumer response to various social content so as to later "replicate the tonality or topic of successful posts."

No. No. No. That is not social. That's direct mail.

Social media are not a place to try to press the right buttons. Such behavior denudes the social space of the very spontaneity and authenticity that powers it. It is not about conquest, any more than friendship is about conquest. It is about shared interests and shared values that can be the basis for priceless but utterly immeasurable lifelong relationships. Customer relations management fits in, the odd offer fits in, but manipulation has no place. The last thing you'd ever want to do is scare people away.

After all, if you insist on getting all quaint about it, an existing customer represents long-term value. A prospective customer has always represented an acquisition cost followed by an unknown. Labor-intensive though it may be, tending to your Venn gardens cultivates your hardiest cash crops while simultaneously planting seeds—at negligible cost—for future harvest. And during that harvest, fresh seeds are scattered by the winds to take root hither and yon. Of course, because it doesn't exist and we can idealize it any way we see fit, we might as well add that NeetFreek spends no money on advertising; it prospers entirely via word of mouth. In fact, it is so beloved, if the customer's friend walks into the customer's kitchen and spies another brand, she gasps with surprise and disappointment.

On that point, once again, we invented NeetFreek for ease of illustration, but let us reiterate that those principles of common ground very much reside in the real world. Such as at that little beverage boutique, whaddya call it . . . ah, yes: the Coca-Cola Co. Successful modern marketing, CMO Joe Tripodi told us, lies in understanding "the marriage between your personal agenda as a brand or a company and the agenda and the interests and the passions of the people around the world you're trying to serve—to find that intersection, that sweet spot, that unique spot where people find an affinity."

Intersecting sets! Well said! Let us toast Joe with a Coke. We'll pour.

Just say Venn.

9

DO'S, DON'TS AND . . . NO, REALLY, *DON'TS*

The longest distance between two points is a shortcut.

—ANONYMOUS

ocial media is many things. Magic isn't one of them. Advertising shouldn't be either. Yet some of the most enthusiastic explorers of the brave new world seem to believe in both. Facebook, Twitter and YouTube are certainly revolutionary channels of communication. But to imagine them as magical ad transporters is simply Consumer Era mentality covered—like something out of *Terminator*—with Relationship Era skin. Recently, for example, one of your authors was reviewing some documents prepared for a client by a prospective agency on the subject of Facebook. Here was one conspicuous sentence: "Marketers are using social media to drive loyalty and repeat transactions." Then came the delineation of a three-point strategy, the first two points of which—cultivating community and conversation—made perfect sense. But not point three: "Convert conversations into transactions that support business objectives."

Yikes. Though designed to reassure clients about the efficacy of social marketing, it was terrible advice. Yes, we are all of us in business with transactions in mind. Yes, more transactions are almost always better than fewer transactions. Yes, we hope our social media efforts—like everything else we do—will be followed by more people purchasing our goods and services. Indeed, if you succeed in forging relationships with your various constituencies, and you are open and honest and share (in both directions) compelling and relevant stuff, loyalty and trust will grow and from that will flow more business at lower acquisition costs. But if you are cultivating community and conversation for the purpose of corralling cattle into the slaughterhouse, you are not engaging in a social strategy. You are engaging in a sales strategy, which is pretty close to the antithesis of social marketing.

We are in the Relationship Era. This is no time for manipulation. If you believe luring friends and confidants to your social space is the right way to set up a business relationship, why take half measures? Join Amway. Don't forget the motivational tapes.

A second client document proposed a content strategy, much of which was dead on. Yet it included a large component of content focusing not on the community, and not on the general concerns of the category, but on the brand itself: What its history is. How to use it. How special it is. Blah. Blah. Blah. You know what that stuff is called? It's called "advertising." Also, when it excessively dominates the conversation, "bad manners." *Welcome to our home! Please be our guest. Let's get to know one another. But first: Let us tell you how great we are. We are soooo great, in the following ways. . . .*

In a social situation, the more you sell, the more you scare—or simply bore—people away. The harder you try to close, the more likely you are to be closed out. This central truth is not difficult for brands to understand, but for some reason it is hard for them to internalize and act upon. What is first required is to embrace social relationship building not as the latest marketing fad, or even as a new reality that has been forced upon you, but as a means to revaluate who you are, what you stand for and why you are in business in the first place. If the only answer is "more transactions," the future will not be kind to you.

Oh, and there is a corollary to that: If you think you are beginning with a clean slate, the *present* will not be kind to you.

Kick Me

Franklin Delano Roosevelt was elected four times to the presidency of the United States. He created the New Deal and presided over the end of the Great Depression. He electrified Appalachia and the nation's spirit. He defeated Hitler. All in all, not a bad resumé. Yet he was one of the most despised American presidents. Nearly seventy years after his death, FDR remains in some quarters synonymous with creeping socialism, sinister Jewish conspiracy and, of course, tyranny. If you were to go on to Twitter seeking commentary on FDR's legacy, you would get a lot of "Our greatest modern president!" and plenty of "Stalin in a wheelchair." It's a big, wide world out there and everyone's got an opinion.

Which should be entirely obvious to any institution about to solicit opinion from the entire connected world. No matter how big and rich you are, you cannot set boundaries around the incoming. In fact, the bigger you are, and the more you have historically dictated your message, the more exposed you are.

Let's imagine, strictly hypothetically, that you were the world's largest Scottish burger chain. Let's further assume that you had built a global colossus by over sixty years feeding ninety-nine billion people fatty, salty, yummy, cheap and quintessentially fast food. You haven't done anything wrong, exactly, but you have been a historic enabler of dietary misconduct on a grand scale—beginning with the tiniest children. Your insatiable requirements for inexpensive beef and soy-based chicken feed have led to deforestation in South America and unleashed greenhouse gases into the atmosphere. Your paper and plastic waste stuffs landfills and your very global expansion is the symbol of plasticized American cultural McImperialism. Let's just say.

So what to do? The first thing, obviously, is to work on these issues, either as a public relations imperative or as an act of good citizenship, or both. Another impulse might be to simultaneously create advertising, socking into that campaign more cash than you've invested in actually addressing the underlying issues. One campaign would bathe ecofriendlier activities in soft focus and warm light, couching them as the generous acts of folks who just plain care. The second would soft focus on your raw materials—the eggs and produce and potatoes—portraying them as the products of God's green earth, delivered to you by sun-drenched rustics in antique pickup trucks just like the families at your local farm stand.

Bullshit, in other words. But it might make you feel better about your industrial self and allow your, ahem, heavy users to buy into the myth. You can do that when you control the message. Nowadays, though, even if you spend $2 billion on advertising worldwide, no message is within your control. Yet decades at the apex of the power pyramid have left you feeling Svengali-like, so comes the Relationship Era and off you go thinking you can keep the *hoi polloi* under your spell. You've been very successful at, for instance, co-opting mom bloggers with free trips and merchandise to tout your advances and good intentions, so why not go to the next level? Why not ask the very public you're trying to influence to provide your best advertising for you? After all, if they are willing to do such things spontaneously, wouldn't they jump at the chance when invited to weigh in?

The answer, of course, is yes. The problem is, as FDR's example demonstrates, the haters will weigh in, too. As they did, most unhypothetically, when on January 18, 2012, the decidedly non-Svengalis at McDonald's sent out a pair of tweets:

"When u make something w/pride, people can taste it,"—McD potato supplier #McDStories http://t.co/HaPM5G9F[1]

Three hours later came a follow-up:

Meet some of the hard-working people dedicated to providing McDs with quality food every day #McDStories http://t.co/ BoNIwRJS[2]

Awwww, what a sweet idea! A Twitter hashtag campaign seeking authentic McDonald's stories! Surely over the years there are literally millions of them, warmhearted tales of romance, adorable kids, camaraderie, safe haven, unexpected reunions, generosity from strangers—the whole gamut of, well, *humanity*. Who doesn't have a story to share? (In fact, one of your authors looks fondly back at the birth of his second daughter. On the day that the newborn and mom were to be picked up at the hospital, he took his eldest girl—then almost three—to McDonald's, where they discussed her new role as big sister. It was, naturally, a preemptive strike by Dad to prepare the no-longer only child for a new reality by lying to her about how important she'd be in the new family. She ate three molecules of her Happy Meal hamburger, took two sips of her orange drink, unwrapped her toy and—whee!—up on dad's shoulders she went as they departed for their new family adventure. Whereupon the child was practically decapitated by the restaurant's ceiling fan. That dad! What an idiot. Just a head bump, as it turned out, but, you know . . . memorable.)

McDonald's would probably have been delighted to see the ceiling-fan story related, compared with some of the other responses tweeted by civilians who gleefully chimed in with McDonald's stories calculated to embarrass the sponsor. So unwarmhearted were the tweets, *Forbes* dubbed the hashtag campaign a "bashtag" campaign.[3] Which, naturally, was its destiny. Note where McDonald's is located on the Brand Sustainability Map.

If that is where you are located on the BSM, a lot of people have issues with you. It is a very good idea to listen carefully to Twitter, et al., to find out what those issues are in order to address them. It is a terrible idea to stage a public rally and randomly hand out bullhorns. Your nastiest critics will grab them, too, and speak right up.

Found a dirty band aid in the bottom of the take out bag. #McDStories[4]

Dude, I used to work at McDonald's. The #McDStories I could tell would raise your hair.[5]

BRAND SUSTAINABILITY MAP

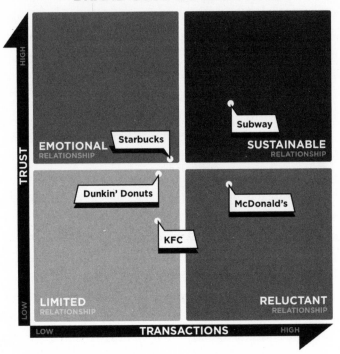

#McDStories Paid for my food but almost left cause I was high and convinced that the workers called the cops and were using my food as bait[6]

Hair in my Big Mac #McDStories

haven't been to McDonalds in years, because I'd rather eat my own diarrhea. #McDStories[7]

Thank you #McDStories you gave me a very valuable lesson for my marketing job today and it was free:)[8]

The last one is our favorite. McDonald's got schooled, too. After quickly pulling the plug on the promoted-tweet campaign, McDonald's social media director took stock, telling the *Los Angeles Times* "We're learning from our experiences."[9] He observed that only 2 percent of the day's #McDStories tweets were negative—but that amounted to fourteen hundred rancid McNuggets feeding the Twittersphere,[10] leading to ritual humiliation in what remains of the old-fashioned unsocial media.

This episode demonstrates why many brands so fear and distrust the Relationship Era in general and social media in particular. The beast can turn on you. You show faith in the public by soliciting authentic stories, and they come back with dirty Band-Aids. Of course, in truth, McDonald's wasn't looking for authentic stories; it was looking for a *selection* of authentic stories, denuded of negativity, for the maximum benefit to the brand. How they imagined the Twitter exercise would yield only p.r.-friendly anecdotes is an absolute mystery. Maybe in Oak Brook, Illinois, everyone believes the McDonald's experience is always like the TV commercials, but nobody else thinks so. Even loyal customers and employees of McDonald's can't be depended on to toe a corporate line. On the contrary, they've seen it all. Familiarity often breeds contempt; it also sometimes breeds admiration and trust. (Weirdly, the blogosphere and Twittersphere are awash in stories all but made to order for a McDonald's stories project. All the brand had to do was tweet and retweet the authentic, organic and positive content already out there.)

Tilting at Epidemics

If sophisticated marketers frequently miss the point of Facebook and Twitter, at least they squander a minimum of time and effort doing so. On YouTube, at significant investment of money and resources, the same titans make fools of themselves every single day.

In the examples above, what marketers imagined was getting free pass-along via Facebook and Twitter for de facto ads. So accustomed are they to manipulating consumers with their ad messages they believe they can manipulate us all into being mules *for* their ad messages. They believe if they can do so on a large enough scale, they can retrieve what they've lost of their beloved reach. Who wouldn't wish to achieve online what TV has so effortlessly provided all these years? It's time to move on, however, and as part of that difficult weaning process, brand stewards should start by putting these out of your mind: Subservient Chicken, Justin Bieber, Old Spice, Susan Boyle, Blendtec Blenders, Rebecca Black, *Charlie Bit My Finger*.

That list, of course, is a gallery of megaviral videos—a very short list of online-sharing phenomena that has encouraged thousands upon thousands of marketers to try to achieve scale by outbreak. Blendtec's videos of the owner grinding up iPhones and so on in his industrial-strength blender has had two hundred million views. *Charlie Bit My Finger*, at this writing, had been seen a half billion times. Justin Bieber alone is closing in on three *billion* YouTube views. Could it be that the Relationship Era enables brands, at minimal cost, to predictably create virtual epidemics of positive buzz?

No.

No, as in "no, no, no and furthermore, no." First of all, Bieber, Black and Boyle are all vocalists; their viral videos are music videos—that is, free performances. The videos do promote the performer's brand, but they are also the product itself. *Charlie Bit My Finger* is a found object, a bit of adorable video serendipity, entirely devoid of commercial intent. Of the top hits, only Blendtec and Burger King's "Subservient Chicken" were branded—and Burger King's results were by no means (as we shall see) fully organic.

As previously noted, according to the viral consultancy Visible Measures, six of seven branded videos—no matter how significantly jump-started with paid "seeding" à la "Subservient Chicken"—fail to amass even 1 million views (i.e., the equivalent of one TV spot airing one time on *CBS This Morning*). Without seeding, 499 out of 500 fail to achieve 500,000 views. No wonder. In that previously mentioned survey conducted by the marketing department of the *New York Times*, consumers were asked to rank five motivations for sharing content. Here's how they voted:

1. To bring valuable and entertaining content to others
2. To define ourselves to others
3. To grow and nourish our relationships

4. Self-fulfillment
5. To get the word out about causes or brands[11]

Rex Briggs, founder of Marketing Evolution, a leading ROI consultancy, says that, in the first place, content created for low-involvement goods has a low probability of being shared at all. "How much content do I need, or am I willing to pass along, related to the ream of paper I buy from Staples?" he asks, rhetorically. But even in high-involvement products, such as automotive, his data show that the pass-along factor hits a wall when the viewer feels a brand is coming on too strong: "At a certain point, 'selling' overwhelms the value of the information/content and pass along begins to drop off. That has less to do with the brandedness, and more to do with the 'no one likes a hard sell' response, known in academic literature as 'counter-arguing,' which is when a person hears a sales pitch and looks to shoot holes in the sales argument."

Further confirmation of the inverse relationship between brandedness and acceptance comes from Thales S. Teixeira, assistant professor at Harvard Business School. He and his colleagues used eye-tracking devices and "zapping" metrics to conclude "consumers have an unconscious aversion to (forceful) brand images, as these are associated with intrusive persuasion attempts." He summarized the results for the Advertising Research Foundation:

Consumers like brands. What they don't like is being sold to, particularly while they are consuming another valued product: entertainment. In a study involving 2000 consumers, my colleagues and I used infrared eye-tracking technology to understand what objects viewers look at and how what they see affects their ad skipping patterns. We found that viewers are more likely to stop watching TV commercials, e.g., switching the channel, at the moment in which brand logos appear on the screen. This effect is not a function of whether consumers like or are familiar with the brand; it happens systematically across brands and people. It is also not the result of the viewer's curiosity being satisfied by the revelation of the brand, as more and more people 'zap out' each additional time the brand appears within the same ad. In addition, longer brand exposures, bigger logos, and logos in the center of the TV screen all contribute to further reductions in viewership. This effect of branding avoidance is so strong that it seems to be incorporated into people's subconscious—they are not aware of their own passive resistance to persuasion.

Yes, people like brands, and they like stuff, and they especially like cool stuff, but they don't like being toyed with even within the context of a TV commercial, so imagine the reaction to a social moment expropriated by commercial interests. Yet there are several entire industries—including the sad, benighted ad-agency biz—that have substantially bet their futures on the ability to defeat not only human nature but the laws of nature as a whole.

Like most every other major issue explored in *Can't Buy Me Like*, online virulence parallels virulence in human terms. It is an epidemiological construct, succeeding or failing based on approximately the same math that dictates the spread of infectious disease in the human population—where, by the way, despite the presence of countless pathogens, rampant infection is an extremely rare event. That happy fact is owing to what is known as the reproduction rate: if every person who comes in contact with an infectious organism—or video—passes it along to one other person, the rate (Ro) equals one. At that rate, the number of infections will grow linearly and very slowly until at some point one infected individual fails to pass it along. Once the Ro is greater than one, there is the possibility for exponential growth—or, as it is called in the world of public health, epidemic. For instance, in an unvaccinated population, the Ro for measles is seventeen. The Spanish flu of 1918, which killed between 3 and 6 percent of the world population, had a Ro of three. The reason we are not all dead from the Ebola virus, which is more than 90 percent fatal and for which there is no practical vaccine, is that it's spread by bodily fluid exchange only and therefore has a Ro safely below one.

There you have it. If you want a "viral campaign," all you have to do to start is create a video that is a lot more contagious than the

Ebola virus. Which is pretty hard when a significant percentage of the time brandedness is an immune-system booster, depressing the *Ro* of a given piece of content. The myth of virality was further punctured by three researchers—Duncan J. Watts, Jonah Peretti, and Michael Frumin—who were seeking answers for *optimizing* video pass-along. They offered a partial solution (seeding, which we will soon address), but first they drew a cold bath:

> The problem, of course, is that designing something to have an R > 1 is no mean feat. Not only must each individual, on average, pass it on to more than one new person—at least one of those people must in turn be motivated to pass it on again, and so on.
>
> Successful infectious diseases all have R > 1, but there are relatively few such diseases, and they are the products of millions of years of evolution and natural selection. Marketers, by contrast, are trying to come up with viral products every day. The chances are, therefore, even talented creatives will typically design products that exhibit R < 1, no matter how hard they try.[12]

If any vendor should claim a special expertise in divining what creative idea will beat the odds, defeat human resistance and rewrite the mathematics of epidemiology, protect your wallet. Also remember the words of legendary screenwriter William Goldman, about Hollywood's utter inability to distinguish a hit from a flop: "Nobody knows anything." You can't catch lightning in a bottle. The key word in "viral phenomenon" is *phenomenon*.

So that's the bad news. The good news is that you don't have to outsmart God to have an impact, or even to attain "free" views among those you most wish to engage.

Johnny Appleseed

"If you have the best content in the world," says Brian Shin of Visible Measures, "imagine that zero people have seen that content, then it has zero chance to get passed along."

Simply uploading a video to YouTube, for instance, creates a natural audience of near zero. Who will find that diamond buried in a Sahara of sand? Posting it on a Facebook page will give it a boost, but the vagaries of the Facebook algorithm militate against a large pool of potential viewers. Therefore, to stimulate the spread of content, marketers are obliged to acquire first-generation viewers in strategically chosen online venues much as they'd make any media buy. In epidemiological terms, this is like sending people infected with Ebola into situations where the virus might spread. That would be called "terrorism." In the online universe, it's called "seeding." Even the most famously viral marketing coups are accomplished in precisely this way, as Watts, Peretti and Fruman reported:

> For example, Burger King's widely admired "subservient chicken" campaign reached millions of viewers, but was also supported by a nationwide marketing effort that yielded a very large seed. Although many people heard about the website through word of mouth, many others saw television ads paid for with a multimillion dollar advertising budget. Perhaps because it makes a better story, journalistic accounts of the campaign usually fail to mention the paid advertising and present the campaign as a purely viral phenomenon.[13]

Since 2009, Visible Measures has tracked seven thousand-plus campaigns adjudged to have achieved some measure of virality. Virtually all were kick-started with an ad buy—a category of spending Shin believes, based on eMarketers' estimate of $3.12 billion for online video advertising, exceeds $600 million annually. "Maximizing pass-along or virality of content," he says, "is really a combination of having both entertaining and targeted content, combined with focusing the distribution and the places where the content can be activated."

Now, Here Are Those Do's We Promised You

So if virality is a lightning strike, why bother purchasing the media to try to trigger it? The answer is subvirality.

Subviral marketing doesn't necessarily seek, quixotically, to send the R_0 factor above one. What it does seek to do is take advantage of pass-along below the threshold of true virality to obtain incremental views in specific communities over and above what are bought and paid for. In other words, bonus views. By increasing the yield of views from 10 to 100 percent, the subviral effect not only increases the ROI of the ad buy, it does so with engaged attention and the trust conferred by pass-along from a friend. Furthermore, even at a relative low absolute reach, Shin says evolving data suggests social viewing may be a key performance indicator for sales. Correlation isn't causation, he says, "but we want to prove that viewership as a form of engagement does directly have value for a brand's KPIs."

He hastens to add, however, that this doesn't mean repurposing a TV spot, putting a seeding budget behind it and expecting to somehow trigger an epidemic. Remember, even Ebola requires the kind of closeness in which fluids are transmitted. The content must be compelling for the communities where it is being introduced. "The human element is the center of everything," Shin says. "The consumer is in control. You have to design a campaign around a user."

If you paid attention earlier, that assertion may strike you as contrary to our premise: that the Consumer Era mentality of pandering to perceived consumer desires must give way to clearly articulated brand purpose. But there is no conflict; content need only make sense in the Venn intersection of brand purpose and audience interests—something advertising seldom does. But if online video isn't a repurposed TV commercial, then what is it? Well, one answer is actual content—the sort of content you for your whole career have placed your advertising *next to*. And we're not necessarily speaking of entertainment content, either. Just think of the vertical channels in magazines and cable that have attracted advertisers targeting certain audience segments since time immemorial. Your video can be just that: relevant, compelling stuff that would be useful—or simply amusing—to those in your spheres of interest.

A fine example is a long-running DIY series of videos created by Betty Crocker. This campaign, you might have noticed, is seldom mentioned alongside Old Spice, Blendtec and other famous case histories. It was not conceived to be sent zipping around the world by office workers under the subject line "OMG! Totally watch this!!!!!" It was created for women who want to make birthday cakes shaped like butterflies, dinosaurs, rubber duckies, castles and other childhood icons. Over the course of five years, the how-to videos have accumulated almost 70 million views on 1,500 different sites.[14] The most popular video—the princess cake—racked up more than 10 million views. As a group, they still generate 135,000 clicks per day.

But Betty Crocker's agency, TouchStorm, didn't do a media buy to acquire seventy million sets of eyeballs. It filmed the videos in Betty Crocker's Minneapolis test kitchens and syndicated the content to publishers, with whom the agency split revenue on a per-click basis. Presumably, few of those seventy million clicks came from folks watching the construction of a rubber ducky cake just for giggles. The majority were there for the instruction. In the print world, such content would be called "advertorial," although the term makes Alison Provost, TouchStorm's founder and CEO, very uncomfortable.

"We call it branded information," she says, "rather than branded entertainment. We don't let them cross the line to selling, but they take the credit for being expert. Brands know stuff. You can have a seventeen-year-old tell you how to curl your hair, or you can have Pantene tell you."

In some categories, not only are the brands experts on the goods they sell, their customers are experts, as well. When Radio Shack turned its back on its traditionally core DIY customers to focus on mobile, it also missed a huge opportunity to coalesce on online community to offer instruction, advice and troubleshooting on all manner of technological questions. In a moment of notable courage, then-CMO Lee Applbaum told the Association of National Advertisers Masters of Marketing Conference that this had been a blunder.

Curate

While creating so-called owned content can be useful, productive and trust enhancing, it can also be expensive, and—due to that expense—marketers tend to err on the side of heavier branding. As we have seen, the more heavy-handed the branding, the more the resistance, and the more likely the content will be seen as thinly veiled advertising—which is less trustworthy even than in-your-face advertising, because of the perception of sneakiness. Would you be more likely to give money to a panhandler or to someone with a probably phony story about leaving her wallet at home?

On the other hand, trust is cumulative. As discussed in the six levels of Venn, goodwill can be accumulated over time by fostering a relationship exactly akin to ones with friends and loved ones. In this context, that means sharing relevant content that may have nothing to do with your brand per se but everything to do with the Venn overlaps of interest between you and your publics. Our friend Steve Rosenbaum, author of *Curation Nation*, is the founder of Magnify.net, a video-hosting platform composed of thousands of highly vertical channels created by brands, publishers and just plain folks interested in, say, hamsters or waterskiing or the paleo diet. Some of the videos to be found on any given channel are created by brands, but most are found objects placed in the channel for the benefit of the community. He wonders, along with us, why more brands don't do the same thing across all their channels of connection with their various constituencies.

"The thing that makes content 'authentic' is the one thing that media creators can't build in a studio or mock up on a sound stage," Steve says. "Authentic video comes from real people. Take 'Charlie Bit My Finger,' a video that's now been seen half a billion times. Charlie is a kid. A real kid. His brother is a real brother. And for all of us who've had to lean over the front seat and threaten 'I'm going to pull this car over if you two don't stop it,' the video hits the spot. It's authentic.

"Can't you imagine a brand like Band-Aid shifting from trying to invent emotional stories in a studio to a new mode of advertising—a model that has them shifting from creating to curating. What if Band-Aid each week combed the web for 'ouchie moments' and then shared the best of the best with Web viewers who were looking for a charming moment of family entertainment. I bet there's a Charlie to be found each week.

"And then Band-Aid could focus on some new target audience, like Xtreme teen sports, gathering a weekly collection of 'Dude, that must have hurt' videos from skateboarders eating asphalt. Nothing extreme, nothing inherently dangerous (that wouldn't be brand-safe). But just some awesome bumps and bruises. If you play the game, and try to imagine just how many brands would benefit from curating authentic content around their 'brand story' the list grows and grows.

"It means inviting your customers to become collaborators in the brand story. Inviting your passionate fans to share videos they've made or discovered—and then curate the best of the best. Brands as curators is sure to be here, and sure to grow, as the evidence mounts that Web video viewers reject glossy, slick, 'corporate' messages, and instead connect with raw, first-person-authored material."

Perhaps you think Steve is just being self-serving, and maybe he is. But you should know something about him. He essentially invented Consumer Generated Video, more than twenty years ago, when he literally mailed digital cameras to teenagers and young adults and asked them to tell their own stories. This led to his pioneering show *MTV Unfiltered*, which was where it all started.[15]

He's not the only one with experience, either. The elder of your coauthors has twin grandsons who, at the age of seven months, had a video posted on YouTube in the aftermath of a particularly unsightly lunch. The twenty-two-second clip opens with a phone-cam view of Oren after a meal of strained blueberries and sweet potato. He's got a shadow of lunch around his mouth, but just a shadow. Basically, he looks like Fred Flintstone. In the background, you hear his dad say, "Oren you're a mess. . . . Actually, you look pretty clean in comparison." Then the proud father pans right to Oscar, whose face is entirely, hilariously smeared, especially his eyebrows.

It looks like a sweet potato mask. Their dad instantly loses it, breaking out in his notably squeaky laugh. Oscar doesn't react, though. He simply stares at the camera, utterly phlegmatic, looking not like Fred Flintstone at all but like Winston Churchill . . . after a pie-eating contest. Meanwhile, the old man is still cracked up. "Oscar," he giggles, "you are *soooo* bad at eating."

That's it, just a messy slice of life that has captured the imagination of one million online viewers—and eventually those of *The Ellen DeGeneres Show* and *Tosh.0*. But of all the untold jillions of baby videos on YouTube, why would this one break out? It's not as though there were a glimpse of Sasquatch in the background, or a kitten on a sliding board. It's just two oddly impassive babies and an unseen cackling dad.

The explanation? Human intervention.

It just so happens that the boys' aunt, Miry Whitehill, is in the video-seeding business. After the kids' mom was persuaded to post the family fave clip on YouTube, Miry got busy. She was curious, she says, for a firsthand glimpse of video sharing minus any brandedness or paid seeding.

"This is the first time I ever distributed one that was just, 'Oh! Look how *cute* this is!'

"It didn't happen in a vacuum," she concedes, but, by the same token, she spent not a dime and called in no favors. "Since I work in the video space, I didn't want to use any professional contacts. I wanted to see what a random person could do with a cute video. I went across every single 'mom blog' that I knew about and started submitting it everywhere."

It has since landed on Yahoo's This Week in MOM; Shine from Yahoo; Lite FM, Chicago; The Hairpin; The Slacker Mom; Rukkle the Midweek Playpen; Funnyjunk.com; The Viral Trend; Nick Mom; Right This Minute; Vidster; and, courtesy of the boys' Aunt Allie, BuzzFeed.com.

Plus Israeli television, naturally.[16]

"It's just this free-for-all Internet lovefest," Miry says, somehow amazed and amused that the virality she is paid to spawn is actually, you know, possible. "It's really, really exciting. I'm a little jealous because Oscar and Oren's resumés are now way more impressive than mine."

One reason she so enjoyed Project Baby Slobs was to investigate, "If you take branding out of the picture, what does that unleash?" The answer turned out to be that a totally Beyonce-and-Sasquatch-less video can so catch on while others, manufactured at significant expense by ad agencies the world over for the explicit purpose of going viral, just languish on YouTube's servers undisturbed. So why are so many creating expensive duds instead of doing exactly what BuzzFeed and Ellen DeGeneres do: scouring the Internet for videos they'd like to share with the communities they are interested in, to share by e-mail, Facebook and even the paid seeding that yields such modest return for owned content. That is the stuff of the Relationship Era; it's not selling, but sharing. It's finding common ground and passing along a funny or relevant video, just like friends do. Also, ahem, the content is free. In the next chapter, you will meet an intrepid banker who launched just such an experiment.

Genuine Naugahyde

The business world is awash in companies and brands that believe they have forged a social strategy, but actually are just selling (and usually being sold) a bill of goods. That's why there is an ever-growing list of hilarious and/or tragic pratfalls resulting from treating social media as a gimmick or a fashion or a fad. Beware: All that Twitters is not gold. As many marketers have discovered the hard way, you can't fake authenticity. The Internet will be on to you in a New York minute. So don't playact at sincerity, don't pander to customers, don't whitewash or greenwash, don't try to purchase goodwill ("For every purchase of Energy Drink, we will donate 10 cents to the Youth Nutrition and Wellness Foundation. . . .") and give serious consideration to telling the truth. All of it. Transparency is disarming. Share with your customers things that you have always obscured—cost structure, for example, or regulatory challenges, or manufacturing errors. In a trust relationship, when the going gets tough, your "members" are willing to give you the benefit of the doubt.

In the event you do commence sharing video, pix, blog items and other mutually relevant content harvested from the Web, do not— repeat, DO NOT UNDER ANY CIRCUMSTANCES—try to pass off a manufactured good as a found object. This seems obvious, as previous purveyors of phony authenticity have paid such a heavy price, yet sordid episodes continue to play out . . . with all the predictable discovery and backlash.

On April 26, 2012, a pair of black buses pulled up in front of the Apple store in Sydney, Australia, and disgorged scores of black-clad protesters with printed signs declaring WAKE UP! The ninja picketers immediately began chanting those words, and other garbled ones, in what has been (inaccurately) described as a "flash mob." Who and what they were demonstrating on behalf of was unclear. As it turned out, though, popular video-blogger Nate "Blunty" Burr was shopping in the Apple store when the episode broke out, and hurried out to gather video of the whole megillah. He posted a blog describing the strange episode he'd serendipitously witnessed and then wondered aloud about who might have been behind such guerilla-marketing tactics.

"What? Why? Who? How?" Blunty posed to his viewers. "What was that about?"[17] Subsequently, the video gathered views as other bloggers began to speculate. Suspicion turned to Samsung before a blogger was able to track some source code in a WakeUp! Web page to RIM, Research in Motion, the makers of BlackBerry. But, wait . . . Blunty had worked closely with RIM in the past. Was he in on the whole stunt?

Yep, and his description of how he just happened to encounter and film the mob, and his assertions of being mystified by the WakeUp! calls, were all part of the plan. In a peevish follow-up post, he castigated other bloggers for passing along rumors, yet somehow failed to castigate himself and RIM for passing along out-right lies.[18] Needless to say, the upshot was a blackberry pie in the face—the latest in a string of RIM social-media blunders, including a bashtag fiasco of its own. Here's how Steve Lundin of Marketing-Nightmares.biz saw the whole shabby WakeUp! affair:

> The Australian marketing nightmare was actually a physical representation of the brand's woes. RIM's fake mob stood outside of Apple's mighty temple, and conducted a demonstration that was as impotent as it was confused. What kind of message does "wake up" send to the market? Were they trying to say that Apple had slipped us a global ruffie and it was time to "wake up" to the reality that we all really wanted Blackberry's again? Is this any different than a cast-off from the first round of American Idol complaining that Beethoven, Charles Mingus and Bruce Springsteen are a bunch of talentless amateurs? RIM is trying to stop a freight train by putting an egg in its path.[19]

It was also taking a path long since discredited by the epic failures of Walmart (Walmarting Across America), Coke Zero (The Zero Movement) and McDonald's (4Railroads). All of those misled consumers into thinking they were seeing something organic and authentic, but delivered only brand-manufactured fraudulence. Watching these scandals periodically emerge is dispiriting, to say the least. Not only do such petit frauds bespeak a widespread misunderstanding of social media, they also miss the vast opportunity for popular brands to succeed by being themselves.

Consider Southwest Airlines—the famously efficient, famously frill-free cattle car that is not afraid to laugh at the air-travel experience and at its own Spartan ways. Late in the winter of 2012, an Austin-bound passenger was amazed by an (apparently) impromptu challenge from two flight attendants named Mandy and LaDonna. The women had handed out barf bags filled with galley items and asked for volunteers to try out airplane-food recipes. Now, Southwest doesn't offer much in the way of food, so the possibilities were

BRAND SUSTAINABILITY MAP

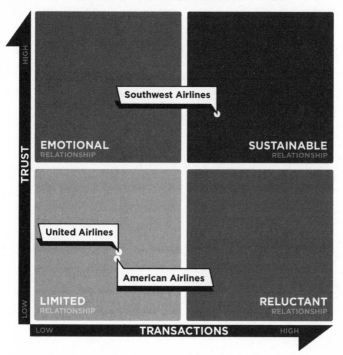

limited—which was the joke of the thing. Thus the passenger—
Laughing Squid blogger Rusty Blazenhoff—was more than amused:

> Mandy called the first recipe "Key Lime Cookie Dough Sort Of"
> and it consisted of crushed airplane-shaped cookies, Coffee Mate
> creamer and a wedge of lime. The next was simply peanut butter
> and several passengers attempted to crush peanuts to a smooth
> consistency. It got even better when the pilot came out and of-
> fered up an unexpected suggestion: Chocolate Mousse. It was a
> simple recipe made of powdered hot chocolate mix and Coffee
> Mate creamer. We ended up dipping our mini pretzels into the
> (somewhat delicious) finished "mousse." Winners were an-
> nounced and much fun was had by all involved. In fact, it may
> have been the most fun I've ever had on a commercial flight.[20]

There is paid media, like advertising; owned media, such as Betty Crocker how-to videos; and earned media—the kind you get when you are noticed from the outside. The Southwest example is therefore very much another "do" among a rogues' gallery of "don't." Because, in general, it is preferable to earn a reputation as a genuine purveyor of fun than as, say, a desperate, lying sack of shit.

10

BANK AND TRUST

Be daring, be different, be impractical, be anything that will assert
integrity of purpose and imaginative vision against the play-it-safers,
the creatures of the commonplace, the slaves of the ordinary.

—CECIL BEATON

ecil Beaton, quoted above, was an accomplished twentieth-
century English photographer and theatrical designer. He is why
the costumes in *My Fair Lady* are not authentic Edwardian period pieces but exotic and sometimes eccentric riffs on contemporaneous fashion. He wouldn't be talked out of his vision and wound
up with an Oscar. Not only did Beaton believe that purpose de-
manded change, change was his purpose; he was an enemy of the
status quo.

You yourself needn't be so militant. After all, change is simply
your destiny. The ground is shifting beneath your feet. The only
question is whether you will be toppled and swallowed up by the
earth, never to be heard from again.

But what if you feel all the rumblings and the rest of your organization does not? What if you embrace change and top management fears the consequences? What can one person do—especially
when he or she is not the boss of bosses? To get more specific, how

does a top manager for one of the most conservative players in a historically stodgy industry find himself trying to shift from one paradigm to another? How does an engineer-turned-logistician-turned-consultant-turned-banker come to challenge the status quo—and his own superiors—to embrace social-media relationship building?

Those answers coming right up, but first this trip down bad-memory lane:

In the fall of 2011, the Bank of America made a perfectly rational decision. After having its $4 billion revenue from debit card transactions halved by the stroke of a presidential pen—as part of the Dodd-Frank Wall Street Reform and Consumer Protection Act—BofA sought to recoup what the new law had erased in capping at twenty-two cents the so-called swipe fees banks charge merchants.

Because the thrust of Dodd-Frank was to protect consumers from having their pockets picked by the opaque machinations of the financial services industry, and because "hidden fees" were among the chief complaints of consumer advocates, the bank publicly announced that going forward it would charge account holders $5 per month to use their debit cards. In writing. In clear language. With a full explanation.

Bank of America may as well have announced, in clear language, that it was sending agents into population centers to contaminate water supplies. And setting fire to kittens along the way. The public reacted poorly.

A twenty-two-year-old Washington, DC, woman named Molly Katchpole started an anti-BofA petition that collected 306,000 signatures within days.[1] Editorials around the nation buried BofA in invective, typified by this headline from Illinois's *State Journal-Register*: "Make Big Banks Pay Price for Their Greed."[2] Five Democratic congressmen asked for a Department of Justice probe. And a U.S. senator advised angry customers to take their business elsewhere.

"Get the heck out of that bank," said Illinois Democrat Dick Durbin in a speech on the Senate floor. "Find yourself a bank or credit union that won't gouge you for $5 a month. . . . What Bank of America has done is an outrage."[3]

That was a particularly cruel rebuke to BofA, since it was Durbin's eponymous amendment to Dodd-Frank that created the swipe-fee cap in the first place. Who knew that Washington was not only against hidden fees but also completely transparent ones announced by press release three months in advance? Just for good measure, another inside-the-Beltway figure showed up on *Good Morning America* to take a twenty-two-cent swipe at greedy bankers: "What the banks are saying is that, rather than take a little bit less of a profit," explained President Barack Obama, "the industry would prefer to charge its customers more."[4]

No surprise then that the industry changed its mind. Several big banks, including Bank of America, announced that no such fee would be imposed after all.

"We have listened to our customers very closely over the last few weeks and recognize their concern with our proposed debit usage fee," said BofA co-COO David Darnell, in a press release thirty days after the original one. "Our customers' voices are most important to us. As a result, we are not currently charging the fee and will not be moving forward with any additional plans to do so."[5]

As Emily Litella would have put it, in Gilda Radner's old *Saturday Night Live* sketches, "Never mind."

The question is: Who was to blame for this fiasco? Was it Congress, for passing the Durbin Amendment or the Federal Reserve for suggesting it? No. Was it customers, who don't want banks to make unseemly profits, but do want a valuable service for nothing? No. Was it Senator Durbin and other opportunistic politicians, who saw an easy target in big banking and unsportingly kicked Bank of America when it was down? Nope. Was it Bank of America, for imposing a fee on users who hate fees?

No, not quite. The blame goes to Bank of America, yes, and the rest of the industry—but not for some tactical error. They're to blame for having conducted themselves in such a way for the previous half century that their postbailout reserve of public trust was exactly zero. Thanks to the grace of providence—plus two presidential administrations interested in unfreezing the entire global financial apparatus—the banks were saved from failure, but they were nonetheless seen by the public to be morally and ethically bankrupt. By the time they started taking away "free" checking (which was never free to begin with, despite the shell game banks have been playing with credulous customers for decades), a mere offer of free checking would have improved their reputations not much at all. By the time they announced the debit card fees, an offer of free kidneys would have improved their reputations not much at all.

Suffice it to say the industry's timing could not have been worse. The financial services sector (or most of it) lost trust at precisely the moment when trust is most important for commercial success and sustenance. As we have seen, historical circumstances have converged to decimate the image-making power of advertising just as the Internet has given the public unprecedented levels of information about corporations and brands. BofA had spent tens of millions of dollars on TV commercials about how deeply it understood its customers. When push came to shove, though, turns out the bank understood them very little, indeed.

Boston, We Have a Problem

One less-than-disinterested observer to the card-fee free-for-all was bank executive Eduardo Tobon, who worked not for BofA but for Sovereign Bank in Boston. To be specific, he was the CEO of the payments division of Santander USA, a Spanish global financial services company that owns the medium-sized regional bank. Tobon's revenues weren't going to take a BofA-scale hit from Durbin, but his division was going to get clobbered. He felt his rival's pain.

"It was a slow motion train wreck that the general public did not fully understand," says the thirty-nine-year-old Colombian. "At the end, BofA was losing billions in revenues. They had to react in some fashion, but it was poorly executed on their part. Trust and relationships are hard to build and easy to lose."

He and his team had a different strategy, about which more later, but the key thing about Tobon and Sovereign's card business is that they were incapable—owing to circumstance, resources and temperament—of operating BofA style. Three years earlier, in the middle of the global financial catastrophe, Santander, then a 25 percent owner, had swooped in to buy the remaining 75 percent of Sovereign for chump change. At about $4 per share, it actually paid less for the three-quarters of the struggling regional than it had spent on the initial one-quarter. Sovereign, which was in extremis till then, thus had behind it the capital reserves of Santander—a bank so conservative it had relatively low exposure to the subprime meltdown.

So Tobon didn't have to act hastily.

He also didn't have the resources to advertise his way out of any outbreak of ill will. The very same conservatism that protected Santander from speculation doom also make it a, shall we say, modest investor into marketing programs. Exceedingly modest. And since Sovereign will eventually be renamed Santander, the appetite for supporting the old brand with paid promotion is more limited still. Though the cards division was essentially a start-up, Tobon's budget for television advertising was zero. His budget for print advertising was near zero. In other words, he couldn't be a Consumer Era marketer if he wanted to be. So, like it or not . . . Hello, Relationship Era!

"I was absolutely forced into it," he concedes. "No question about it."

No, Tobon was not, strictly speaking, a visionary. Nor was he a Doug Levy type, who was drawn to relationships and purpose in an honest-to-god conversion experience as spiritual as it was intellectual. In this case, he was more like the engineers at Johnson Space Flight Center when Apollo 13 got into trouble. Given a box full of parts accessible to the astronauts in the crippled spacecraft, they were told to jerry-rig a working compressor. Tobon's box of parts consisted of existing customers, a modest budget for contests and similar brand promotions, traditional market research and a whole assortment of social media. So he commenced to tinkering.

Making a virtue of necessity, they call that. But here's where the temperament factor comes in. Tobon came to the hidebound culture of banking from an unorthodox route. Trained as an engineer, he began his career designing not factories as he'd imagined but supply chains . . . for Procter & Gamble in Latin America. The experience got him interested in business, and his next move was an MBA at Carnegie Mellon in Pittsburgh, Pennsylvania. From there he landed in consulting and client work for a (then) fast-growing regional bank called Sovereign. When he presented his final report to his client on building infrastructure for the recently acquired corporate banking business, he was asked to come aboard as an employee and execute. By training and now by gathering experience, the guy was a problem solver. They offered him salary plus options. So, suddenly he was a staid, dark-suited banker—except, as it turns out, with MacGyver's brain.

"What I learned in engineering has helped me a lot for the rest of my career," he says, "because it is that sort of ingenuity and creativity that I apply in the business world."

His initiative was successful. And so was his next, building merchant services. And his next, a payroll business. And his next, health savings accounts. The projects came fast and furious, the last of which was a survey of the Hispanic market. It was a fateful assignment. His bullish report led to the original 25 percent sale to Santander. Alas, what led to the other 75 percent sale was the global financial crash, in which the high-flying Sovereign lost 80 percent of its market cap. In 2008, after six years, Tobon was a successful executive with brand new management and a safe-deposit box filled with suddenly worthless stock options. The bank was saved. He was wiped out.

"I'll be very honest, I did think many, many times to just basically cut my losses and move on and go into the next thing."

But the new owners liked him. They liked the fact that he was the highest-ranked Hispanic in the bank and they especially liked his track record at building infrastructure and profitability, where there had been little or none. They had an idea to consolidate credit cards, debit cards and merchant services into a single payments division and asked him to run it. And though it was sticky with broken eggs, he decided to stay in the Sovereign basket. Congratulations, Eduardo Tobon! You have lost most of your net worth, the new owners are launching essentially a start-up with no marketing budget. The government is trying to regulate you back to the Stone Age. There are layers and layers of bureaucracy to navigate, and corporate politics on a global scale. And as CEO of payments, you still have to work hand-in-glove with the marketing department of the retail bank, where they have a certain way of doing things that does not necessarily comport with your engineering-informed way of doing things. Have fun!

"The way I was looking at it to probably give myself some peace of mind is, 'I'm running a start-up inside a company and the good news is there is plenty of capital and there are resources available.' And what's the downside? The downside in a situation like that is you can fail miserably and your career can be done with this institution and you might damage your reputation. But the up side can be enormous."

Tobon's journey to Relationship Era practices began through a hire of a junior executive who had interned at MOFILM, a crowdsourcing ad agency. Tobon had never heard of it—or the process of posting ad briefs to the crowd to see what the world of amateurs, semipros and freelancers could come up with. The notion fascinated him, because it meant a brand could produce a TV spot for 5 percent of the ordinary cost and distribute it essentially for free. With this new channel in the back of his mind, he commenced to building his payments team.

MacGyver . . . or Maverick?

"A year later, I feel that I have the team and I'm ready to take on relationship marketing," says Tobon. "I went back to marketing and I said, 'I'd like to create a YouTube channel and start putting some content on it.'"

He might as well have said, "I'd like to shoot $100 bills out of a cannon over the city of Boston." YouTube is the Wild West, and banks tend not to be wild sorts of institutions. Certainly not this bank.

In some ways, oddly, Santander is a proto–Relationship Era marketer. All over the world it has depended on relationships forged at the branch to build loyalty and lifetime customer value. That's why, while virtually every competitor has sought to cut costs by moving banking to ATMs, online hubs and mobile apps, Santander is doubling down on its branch network. On the other hand, to the top management, social media was an inscrutable unknown, more likely to create a scandal than generate profit. Bank employees have no access to social sites at work, so there would be no way to monitor one owned by the company.

Unsurprisingly, he says, "The answer was 'No, you cannot do that.' So I had to fight tooth and nail."

In time he prevailed. Through MOFILM he solicited video spots around the theme "Every statement tells a story." This exercise yielded a charming, funny and wholly unexpected video titled *The Keeper*, about the fictional Gordon Belker, a man who documents his entire life with his debit card statements. It is better than 90 percent of the financial services commercials you have ever seen. (Indeed, the Bob Garfield half of us—a twenty-five-year veteran of advertising criticism—was bowled over when he happened upon the video at the 2011 Cannes Lions International Festival of Creativity. Indeed, he presided over the judging panel that awarded *The Keeper* the agency's top prize. It was a fateful encounter eventually leading to Bob's affiliation with MOFILM's crowd-sourcing competitor, GeniusRocket, and to an advisory role to none other than Eduardo Tobon of Sovereign Santander. So, yes, the hero of this chapter is also our client.)

Tobon took *The Keeper*, which cost him $4,500, and put it up on his new YouTube channel, which cost him nothing. He spent less than $25,000 to seed it strategically online. At this writing, the spot has garnered more than 359,000 views—the very definition of a subviral success. He was intrigued, and other experiments followed.

"There is a company in Boston called Campus Live. Campus Live started as a similar Facebook start-up and are trying to connect folks at campuses and put some gaming around their interactions," Tobon says. "So they started putting games in front of the students and creating a community, which they have successfully built. Not to the degree of Facebook, but they have significantly created a community. So we invested very little money to create an experiment with them. Instead of sweepstakes, which we had done a few of with customers, they went in and said, 'What if we were to walk students and other folks in the community through a series of steps including sweepstakes where you swipe your card and see if you win coffee for a year or pizza for a year or one of six choices?' And it turned out to be so successful that now the bank and all of the departments want to use this for customer acquisition."

None of these projects was without risk. The Madrid global management wished for him to concentrate 100 percent on his P&L instead of distracting himself with dubious New Age gimmicks, but they forgave him as long as he made his numbers. In Boston, where he was obviously less out of sight and out of mind, his political problems were thornier. More than once he'd been told that he would be given latitude, but he was jeopardizing his career. The Campus Live project made his colleagues particularly nervous.

"At the beginning, nobody wanted to touch it; it was too convoluted. 'Why are you dealing with a startup that doesn't have the legal department in place to deal with us?' But if you don't invest in these experiments, in my mind, when you do need them it takes you so much longer to know which ones work and how to create scale with them."

Still, even getting approval for a Facebook page was a prolonged effort, sometimes bordering on the absurd. Due to worldwide Santander policy, bank employees were blocked from social media— even those who would be monitoring and programming the page. At this writing, he had yet to secure permission for the Facebook team to have access to Facebook—with each phone call and e-mail burning a bit more of his significant but diminishing political capital. Imagine if they knew that he'd instructed the ad agency planning the Facebook page to be less promotional with the content, should it ever see the light of day.

"I believe Facebook can provide a platform to have a genuine interaction with your customers and build stronger relationships and trust over time," he explains. "If you're not authentic, people see through it."

Mind you, this is not a social-media guru speaking those words. It's an engineer/supply-chain manager/banker whose only responsibility, in his manager's eyes, is to contribute right now to shareholder return. "We tend to be short-term results oriented mostly around profits," he says. "Over time, I have learned that I need to feed the short-term oriented monster in order to work on the things that I believe will provide the long-term benefits. Ultimately, I cannot claim to have all the answers since I am learning as we speak. It has made me realize how challenging it can be to be truly genuine inside a corporate and marketing culture that has no patience for building long-term sustainable relationships."

But count him as a convert. "The more I learned about [social media], the more I became a believer. If I had to start a new company, even if I had the capital to invest heavily in marketing, I wouldn't do it any other way. And I think that is very much a Eureka! moment that sometimes you come opportunistically into the situation like I did."

Banker, Client, Pioneer

Earlier we talked about the effect of brandedness on social pass-along. We quoted Steve Rosenbaum about the benefits of curation over wanton creation. We told the story of babies Oren and Oscar, who got a million-plus video views with minimum seeding at no expense. We talked of the mounting evidence of an inverse relationship between branding and social sharing. Oddly, or perhaps not so oddly, there has been no definitive scholarship on that question—perhaps because there has been no obvious candidate to underwrite the experiment.

Until Eduardo Tobon underwrote the experiment.

Over long conversations about conventional wisdom in marketing, Tobon realized the opportunity suggested by Oscar and Oren. What if instead of seeding *The Keeper* and other commissioned ads,

Sovereign were simply to pass along video harvested from the Internet on subjects of mutual interest to the bank and actual, whaddya call them, human beings? In that Venn overlap are some fairly compelling subjects: money, spending, credit cards, deals, and so on. So, which would perform better, the ads—or consumer-generated videos with no branding whatsoever, that were simply passed along by Sovereign Santander as a friend would share with a friend?

In the balance, he understood, hangs nothing less than the future of advertising. If in a sharing world humans connect with brands that behave like likeable other humans, a lot of advertising will be displaced by user-generated content. A *lot* lot. Thus, with us whispering in his ear, Tobon agreed to pay for an A/B test putting an equal amount of seeding investment against six videos—three created by his agencies, three just plucked from YouTube. The only branding on the "found objects" would be a red perimeter announcing who had passed it along. The two sets were placed in demographically equivalent sets of online outlets.

We brought in Miry Whitehill, the very same video-seeding expert who had launched the messy twins into stardom, to run the project. The video seeding firm Giant Media was hired to distribute the content in late July 2012 and everybody held their breath. If the YouTube material outperformed the ads, online video marketing would be turned on its ear.

The Tobon Test

The results were apparent on the very first day, when the three Sovereign Santander video ads were outperformed by a two-year-old filling her baby cart at Trader Joe's; a stop-action animation using coins and bills; and, of course, a cat playing with chocolate "gold coins." The only brand message on all three: "Shared with you in mind, from your friends at Sovereign | Santander." From the outset, the user-generated content yielded more initial views than the agency-created ads—even the extremely well-produced spot about a poor schnook being tormented by a devilish Red Spandex Man who repeatedly, hilariously punishes the hero for all his minor transgressions. Notwithstanding the entertainment value and production values of the actual ads, the videos plucked from YouTube generated more viewer comments, more tweets and more shares. Those trends held out through the entirety of the two-week test.

Then, in the category of "no good deed goes unpunished," things got a little weird.

First, it came to Tobon's attention that Giant Media had, with no disclosure whatsoever and certainly no permission, purchased hundreds of thousands of seeding views, not on the premium sites it named in its proposal, but on a social-gaming site call SwagBucks, which pays users in game credits and points toward gift cards for sitting at their screens clicking on video ads. In the seeding business, that is called "incentivized viewing" and is favored by the likes of Giant because audience demographics are easily controlled and the price of such views is very low. By buying at SwagBucks, Giant was paying five cents per view and being paid twelve cents.

In terms of the reach and targeting of his media buy, over two weeks and 670,000 views, Tobon had gotten approximately what he paid for. But with respect to the experiment—that is, the entire purpose of the exercise—the whole lot of us were blindsided. Giant claimed that the viewing behavior of incentivized viewers exactly paralleled the rest of the population, but refused either to release the details of the ad buy or to break out results confirming that the experimental data were consistent across the board. Such is the sketchy world of the fledgling seeding industry and let the buyer beware. For all the world we'd like to exchange high-fives, bask in triumph and declare once and for all that (1) brandedness inhibits engagement and (2) curation stimulates it. Let's just say that the data submitted by Giant, contaminated or not, suggests nothing whatsoever to discount our hypothesis. On the contrary.

One thing the test proved for certain: The curation process can yield astonishing dividends. Three days into the test, Tobon received an e-mail from *Good Morning America*. They wanted permission to show the shopping-baby video for its audience of four million people. Yes, with no intervention whatsoever, history was repeating itself; just like messy eaters Oren and Oscar, the mini grocery shopper was poised to go from online to TV. Needless to say, the bank was in a tizzy. The CMO got involved. The head of digital got involved. E-mails were exchanged. Meetings were taken. Did the bank truly secure the rights? (Answer: yes.) Should GMA be asked to credit the bank? (Answer: no. That would almost certainly be a deal breaker.) Oh my God, *what could go wrong?!?!* Even if GMA never mentioned the bank, the video's appearance would increase by some significant multiple the online views, and the sharing that goes with it. Which is precisely how videos *do* go viral.

Whereupon Eduardo Tobon, maverick banker and wanna be social mediator, was struck by the second bizarro eventuality. His superiors looked at the GMA publicity windfall and said no, thank you. In July 2012, Spain's faltering economy was in the news, the banking sector was under fire, and the brass wanted to stay below the radar. If morning TV watchers were to see a cute little girl shopping adorably and somehow were to connect that warmth and good feeling to Santander, and the same video were to fly around the Internet courtesy of Santander, *people might notice the company!* Yes, Tobon says, his management was afraid of any message they could not control. Because, dear God, what if someone were to see that mini shopping cart and associate it with Spain's shrinking economy or anything else conceivably negative about the past, present or future of Santander, banking, Spain, Europe or the Milky Way galaxy? THEN WHAT WOULD THEY DO?

What Eduardo Tobon did was start answering calls from headhunters. He is now the president of Diner's Club International, where—per the demands and opportunities of the Relationship Era—you can be fairly certain the word *club* will from this point forward be taken very seriously.

11

THIS COULD BE THE END OF A PREVIOUSLY VERY GOOD RELATIONSHIP

For Brutus, as you know, was Caesar's angel: Judge, O you gods, how dearly Caesar loved him! This was the most unkindest cut of all.

— WILLIAM SHAKESPEARE

Name the most successful marketer of the past thirty years. Is it Apple? Nike? Starbucks? Absolut vodka? Virgin Air? It's a subjective matter, but you can make a strong argument for none of the above. You have to consider at least one brand that sells no product at all, except possibly hope: Susan G. Komen for the Cure.

Founded in 1982 by Nancy Brinker, the sister of breast cancer victim Susan Komen,[1] the charity grew to become a fund-raising colossus, raking in $439 million in the 2010–2011 fiscal year.[2] Over three decades, it has provided almost $2 billion for breast cancer research, education, advocacy, health services and social support programs in more than 50 countries. Its pink ribbon is ubiquitous and synonymous with the fight against breast cancer, becoming a symbol of such unquestioned good that commercial brands invested large sums just to be associated with it. These range from Yoplait yogurt to Major League Baseball, American Airlines to KFC,

Smith & Wesson(!) to "Promise Me," the "scent of compassion and courage" flogged on the Home Shopping Network. The licenses alone brought in more than $35 million a year in fees, not to mention the exposure they provided for the 130-plus Komen races held annually around the world. In 2010, there were 60 such partnerships.

In 2009, Brinker won the Presidential Medal of Freedom.[3] Komen for the Cure was ranked no. 2 among nonprofits by the Harris Poll in "brand health." It was among the most trusted institutions in one of the society's most trusted sectors.

Then the ribbon unwound.

In January 2011, Komen announced it was withdrawing grants to Planned Parenthood for breast cancer screenings.[4] Planned Parenthood, of course, has long been a target of social conservatives, whose indignation had recently turned toward Komen as well. There was talk among evangelicals of expressing their displeasure with their feet, not only by running away from the Race for the Cure but loudly boycotting it. The Komen pullout from Planned Parenthood was therefore widely interpreted as craven submission to political pressure—which, if true, was out of character for an organization so associated with female courage. As events unfolded, it emerged that Komen's brand-new senior vice president for public policy, Karen Handel, had been a Republican gubernatorial candidate in Georgia who had herself campaigned on a vow to eliminate state funding to Planned Parenthood. Handel denied a political agenda, but nonetheless quickly "resigned." Komen canceled its decision to rescind Planned Parenthood grants, but that was too little, too late. To the faithful, trust had been breached. The year's Harris brand-health polling happened to fall in the middle of the hubbub, and Komen's ranking plummeted to fifty-sixth. Social media went predictably off the hook, as the *New York Times* put it, "with head-snapping speed." Among the most common Twitter phrases: "I will never donate again."

These apparently were not idle threats. Come spring, races for the cure in Indiana, California, Michigan, Florida, Arizona and elsewhere around the nation reported 15 to 30 percent drops in participation and proceeds.

"We had a community that was glued together," Komen's Arizona spokeswoman Gillian Drummond told *USA Today.* "Suddenly overnight, politics divided them."[5]

And, but for Komen's reserve of trust three decades in the accruing, it could have been worse. A 2011 study in the *Journal of Consumer Psychology* by Shirley Y. Y. Cheng, Tiffany Barnett White and Lan Nguyen Chaplin concluded that consumers tend to react to criticism of their most admired brands as a personal attack on themselves, and typically circle their emotional wagons around the brand under siege. Yes, when under assault, Susan G. Komen and, say, Starbucks, enjoy the same reflexive defensiveness from their faithful as, for instance, the Dallas Cowboys or children under arrest or the state of Israel enjoy from theirs. Giving up on those you believe in is not easy to do. Trust confers a cushion against p.r. blows. When Toyota admitted manufacturing shortcuts leading to an unprecedented series of recalls in 2010, the company suffered minimal consequences. Established trust goes a long way to cushioning brands from bonehead decisions and even scandal. But a cushion is not the same as body armor. It does not protect any institution from the fusillade of ill will that comes with acts of moral lapse. The odd management blunder or product recall is easily forgiven. Hypocrisy and betrayal are not.

When it was revealed in August 2012 that a corporate lobbying campaign against Proposition 37—a California ballot initiative seeking to mandate labeling of genetically modified foods—was being bankrolled by the parent companies of such whole-grained brands as Kashi, Muir Glen and Horizon Organic, the backlash was swift and angry. NaturalNews.com, among others, called for a boycott against the antilabelers. One of the more ominous online comments, from Diane Schrum of Illinois State University, stated the dynamic quite simply: "Read, join, and spread the word."

Or consider Johnson & Johnson. Here is the maker of baby shampoo and a host of other iconic products that actually generate warm fuzzies around the world, a company that enhanced its famous trustworthiness exponentially in 1982, by recalling every bottle of Extra-Strength Tylenol from the shelves—at a cost of hundreds of millions of dollars—after a sociopath stalked retail aisles, lacing some capsules with cyanide. The reserve of trust gathered in this episode is the stuff of marketing history, enshrined in the annals of crisis management and virtually synonymous with the notion of corporate responsibility. As recently as 2010, J&J was recognized by the Reputation Institute as the most reputable U.S. company.[6] Well, that was then. This is now. In the space of two years, three decades of reputation equity has been tarnished by a streak of corporate *ir*responsibility—much linked to the ignoble realities of cost cutting, but some to proactive greed. Recalls of many over-the-counter products over quality problems, including factory contamination. Illegal marketing of prescription drugs. A bribery scandal in China. Medicaid fraud in Texas. Faulty medical devices. Suppressed data. Plant closures on health and safety concerns. Selling products overseas that were banned as unsafe in the United States. It has all added up to gradual slippage of public confidence. In the 2012 Reputation Institute survey, the perennial no. 1 had slid to no. 3.[7]

What seems odd at first blush is how gradually the metrics have come to reflect the erosion of confidence in J&J. no. 1 to no. 3? Not exactly excommunication from the pantheon. Yet the nonprecipitousness of the slide does not discredit the primacy of trust. Here again, accrued goodwill buys a substantial benefit of the doubt. Thus J&J has continued to dine out on its reputation equity. But as the bad news has accumulated, the reserve has dwindled on the way to being expended altogether.

And it can happen to anyone.

Just Sew It

Earlier we met Dara O'Rourke, associate professor of environmental and labor policy at the University of California, Berkeley. He is the founder of GoodGuide, the rater of consumer goods on health, environmental and societal criteria. He is also something of a muck-raker, and, in 1997, he raked all sorts of muck at the Vietnam facto-ries manufacturing shoes and apparel for Nike.

Crikey! Nike! The Swoosh. Michael Jordan. Inspiring and funny commercials. Just Do It. This was one of the handful of brands in history that created vast wealth not on the basis of its ordinary products but on the basis of its extraordinary marketing image, and suddenly the image was undermined. O'Rourke found low wages, enforced overtime, underage labor and dangerous working conditions—including high concentrations of toxic chemicals in the air. The *New York Times* reported his findings and suddenly the brand synonymous with athletic grit, emotion, passion, virtuosity and drama was synonymous instead with sweatshops.

"The real impact was not so much on sales of Nike shoes," O'Rourke says, "but a threat to Nike's brand reputation. For the first time, the brand that spent $1 billion a year promoting and crafting its image was vulnerable."

The company didn't help itself by initially questioning the fair-ness of the criticism. A Nike executive, Vada Manager, infamously pushed back by observing "There is a growing body of documenta-tion that indicates that Nike workers earn superior wages and man-ufacture product under superior conditions."[8] Eventually, Nike replaced argumentative rhetoric with promises to fix the problems, replacing the rhetoric in turn with actual effort and over fifteen years has made dramatic progress. Today GoodGuide rates it an aggre-gate 6.6 in the activewear category. (Patagonia is 8.2. Tony Hawk brings up the rear at 3.9.) Because the company had no choice. There was too much at stake, and no place to hide.

"They'd become the poster boy for sweatshops," O'Rourke says. "Lost sale, or fines from the government, or a lawsuit here and there: absolutely insignificant. But undermining their brand, that's tens of billions of dollars. That's the whole game."

Weirdly, O'Rourke is seeing the game being played out once again. And it ain't déjà vu.

Paging Isaac Newton

More than once in this book, we've invoked the shining example of Apple. We are hardly alone in recognizing the company as having so well fulfilled Steve Jobs's vision of creating beautiful, intuitive technology that works that it has become an industrial colossus and symbol of Excellence with a capital E.

In the first quarter of 2012, the company recorded profits of $13 billion on revenues of $46.3 *billion*.[9] Yes, $13 billion in profit, equal to Google's purchase price of Motorola Mobility, Utah's 2013 state budget, the cost of the 2012 London Summer Olympics and the entire Marshall Plan. In cash. In three months' time. This windfall helped Apple's stock price, which surged enough to nudge the company past a little boutique called ExxonMobil as the largest industrial corporation in the world. No wonder then that in the same week President Obama, in his State of the Union Address, singled the company out as emblematic of all we as a nation should aspire to:

> You see, an economy built to last is one where we encourage the talent and ingenuity of every person in this country. That means women should earn equal pay for equal work. It means we should support everyone who's willing to work, and every risk-taker and entrepreneur who aspires to become the next Steve Jobs.[10]

Now, the mood in Washington is such that if Obama admires the weather, the Republicans will disagree; they will call the weather a path toward socialism. Not that night, however. In the GOP response to the president's address, Indiana governor Mitch Daniels got his licks in, but he also raced to bow at the altar of the sainted one.

> Contrary to the President's constant disparagement of people in business, it's one of the noblest of human pursuits. The late Steve Jobs—what a fitting name he had—created more of them than all those stimulus dollars the President borrowed and blew.[11]

Meanwhile, at almost exactly the same time that leaders of both major parties were tossing laurels at the heroic vision and economic impact of Steve Jobs, there were "new developments" unfolding. One of those developments was a series of *New York Times* articles documenting how Apple's manufacturing jobs—seven hundred thousand of them—are provided by contractors overseas, chiefly in China, and how workers there labor for long hours at vanishingly low wages in hazardous conditions. Then came a long segment on the radio program *This American Life* by monologist Mike Daisey, who had infiltrated an Apple contract-manufacturing plant in the Chinese factory city Shenzhen to find out where his iPad came from. His piece reported inhuman dormitory conditions, a brutal shop floor and a huge net dangling over the shop floor to stem the tide of worker suicides. The impact was blunted somewhat two months later, when Daisey acknowledged embellishing the sufficiently grim facts with fabrications—about child laborers, for instance. What Daisey explained as the prerogative of the artist in the service of greater truth everyone understood to be big fat lies and *This American Life* retracted the episode. But the damage was done. Within two weeks of the initial airing, Apple was obliged for the first time to reveal its Asian subcontractors. Foxconn, the factory owner in Shenzhen, also immediately agreed to boost wages 25 percent.

In the Relationship Era, your every action, and inaction, is advertising.

The evils of Chinese manufacturing, of course, are not unique to Apple. The same factories churn out electronics for Dell, Acer, Lenovo, Nintendo, Panasonic, Samsung, IBM, Cisco, Motorola, Amazon and so on. Furthermore, over time, such enterprise will create a middle class in China, and other developing countries, helping to eradicate grinding property—and to make new markets for our own export goods. But Daisey was nonetheless right in the larger sense: Apple and the rest are lowering costs by using foreign workers in conditions we wouldn't tolerate in our own prisons. One can argue—and your coauthors certainly have, heatedly—about whether this story exemplifies corporate malfeasance or merely the evolution of capitalism in developing countries. Clearly, the reality in China has components of both exploitation and opportunity. But for Apple's circumstances, the argument is immaterial. What is material is that the company was thrust into the center of an international controversy. The heroes of free enterprise—the industrial sweetheart with 3.27 million spontaneous declarations of love— were caught, Red China-handed, being themselves. Remember, in the Relationship Era, your every action, and inaction, is advertising. You'll recall the experiment from Chapter 2. Google "I Love Apple" and you get north of 3 million hits. In the aftermath of the Foxxcon revelations we Googled "Apple China." In the middle of the uproar, we got 412 million results, many from blog posts. One of them looked like this:

"I don't think I will be an Apple customer anymore! I would rather [use] inferior technology."

The headline on the post? "Apple sucks!"

Since then there have been a series of fresh controversies: a U.S. Department of Justice case brought against Apple and major publishers alleging collusion in the pricing of e-books, ragged performance of the Siri voice-command function on the iPhone 4S, an International Trade Commission finding that Apple was infringing on a Motorola patent, resentment from customers about a stock buyback program that enriched investors but left consumers of the pricey gear feeling exploited, and accusations that the new app subscription service was gouging publishers by demanding a 30 percent commission to participate. In June 2012, a report from an NGO called China Labor Watch documented working conditions of the Foxxcon kind, and worse, in Apple-contracted factories throughout southern and eastern China.[12]

"They're having a Nike moment," says O'Rourke—one perhaps all the more threatening, because Apple historically has been notoriously locked down. Steve Jobs, more than any politician, was able to control the message. But it does not control this one. "Apple is the most secretive consumer product company in the world, but over the last year we've seen a lot of cracks in the brushed aluminum and glass façade. The only threat to Apple sales is public trust. Dell doesn't have a chance against them. HP doesn't have a chance against them. HTC doesn't have a chance against them. The only threat to their sales is how they handle these issues.

"We see on their Apple fan sites Apple fanboys saying this is the thing that can turn them away from Apple. This is the threat to their brand and their long-term value. This is the thing that can take them down."

No company is immune to the loss of trust, any more than anything is immune to gravity. Please note that Isaac Newton finally understood that law of nature when he witnessed a falling apple.

For our part, we are optimistic. The company's response—unprecedented disclosures about its supply chain, pressure on subcontractors and a very public mea culpa—suggests it well understands both the repercussions to its brand and the essential human stakes. A July 2012 report from the Fair Labor Association, a consortium of universities, NGOs and corporations dedicated to workers' rights, found that Apple and Foxxcon had rapidly addressed 195 of 195 recommendations from the FLA's scathing earlier findings. "The verification confirmed that Apple and Foxconn are ahead of schedule in improving the conditions under which some of the world's most popular electronics are being made," wrote FLA president Auret van Heerden. "Apple and Foxconn's progress since the March assessment, combined with the additional actions planned through July 2013, would create the road map for all Chinese suppliers in the tech industry." Here, too, we seem to be witnessing a replay of the Nike scandal of fifteen years earlier. In the crucible of international condemnation, after initial reluctance, that company changed its ways. Its dominance as a brand has long since been restored.

Google "I hate Nike." Twenty-nine thousand hits. Google "I love Nike."

A million.

DOUG LEVY

Many who know me consider me annoyingly optimistic. Fortunately, my wife, Alyce, keeps me in check. For years, she has heard me talk about the power of capitalism to improve humanity and how marketing, rooted in purpose, can be the way to bring more profit and more meaning to the practice of business. When I talk about these things, she usually giggles. Once I found on the fridge a note Alyce had left for the babysitter:

"If I don't answer my cell, call Doug. He always has his cell phone with him because he doesn't want to miss a single minute of changing the world through marketing."

Har-dee-har har.

Truthfully, it has been a journey. Intellectualizing the Relationship Era and truly living it did not happen together. Several years ago, there was a senior employee who came to my office at the end of the day and told me that he was planning to leave, a departure that I figured would set the company back six to twelve months. Determined not to let this happen, I called a meeting with my business partner, Marc Blumberg, and my friend and trusted adviser, Rand Stagen. I started the meeting by stating my goal of keeping this employee here. From this group, I needed some help figuring out the right strategy to persuade him to stay.

Persuade him to stay. The irony cannot be lost on you. You've just read eleven chapters about how persuasion is dead.

My partners understood. Rather than a meeting to accomplish my stated objective, I quickly became the subject of an intervention. Marc and Rand called me out on my arrogance and asked why I knew more than this employee about where he should work and whether convincing him to stay would really serve him or us. Was persuasion, they challenged, really the right approach?

Later that night, I found myself on the cold tiles of my bathroom floor, sweating profusely, my head in a tailspin. It had hit me.

I had given thought to the benefits of the fundamental shift from persuading to building authentic relationships. I had even developed proprietary terminology, models, and data to support the concepts. But, something different happened in this moment. I myself had not made the shift. As my friend Rick Voirin once told me, there are some problems you can't think your way out of.

So a late-night "aha" was part of what led to this book. But, only part. I had been talking to my colleagues for years about our purpose, to advance relationships, and my vision for an approach and work product that dramatically elevates both meaning and results for the people we work with.

I was determined to have our purpose inform everything we did. Sure, within a few months of clarifying our purpose, everybody in the agency could dutifully recite the agreed-upon language, but—as the team subsequently experienced with our clients—talking the talk didn't necessarily lead to walking the walk. Evidence that the agency had genuinely internalized the stated core purpose was elusive. That lack of connection between an earnestly described purpose and the daily actions of the company was frustrating for me and for others in the company. I believed we would benefit by that connection and was aggravated that we weren't there. And, no doubt our staff was discouraged about me talking about the purpose with no idea about what to do with it.

Perhaps my late-night conversion was part of what freed the

company to bring the reality of our work into closer alignment with our ideals. And we remain on that path.

Though my name is alongside Bob's on the cover, the concepts and experiences relayed by this book represent the contributions of an exceptional staff at MEplusYOU and an amazing group of friends.

Mark McKinney is the primary author of Marketing with Purpose, our methodology for creating purpose-inspired work. Mark has done what escaped me for years in providing a clear road map by which our team can execute Relationship Era work. Marc Blumberg was an early contributor to the Relationship Era thinking and has led its integration into our work. He has been an exceptional lifelong business partner and friend. Ian Wolfman's enthusiasm for this work has propelled it. Through conference presentations and conversations with top industry leaders, he has tested these concepts in market and helped us refine them. He brought Bob and me together. And, like Marc, Ian has been an exceptional lifelong business partner and friend. Michael Davis and his team of creatives turn words on a piece of paper to brilliant Relationship Era creative executions. Many others have been critical to developing these concepts and bringing them into our work and out to the world, including Bonnie Sayers, Rahul Purini, Tim Rumpler, Jana Boone, and Angie Byrnes. Evelyn Henry Miller, and Heath Wade have built an infrastructure that supports us in delivering purpose-inspired work. Rand Stagen is an extended part of the MEplusYOU family. He has been a soul mate on my journey and a key contributor to the concepts in this book.

BOB GARFIELD

Me, I try to stay off the bathroom floor, unless I've dropped a Lipitor. Doug and I came to the Relationship Era from very different paths. For me, this book fulfills a responsibility to be more than a doomsayer.

My previous book, *The Chaos Scenario*, was an apocalyptic warning about the collapse of mass media and mass marketing. Indeed, if I do say so, it was uncannily prescient in describing the disruptions so confounding to marketers today. The book did promise days of milk and honey to come, but apart from describing the advantages of social listening, the benefits of social sharing and the gold mine of social advocacy, it was thin on specifics. It was sparing on examples. And it was barren of practical advice.

Mind you, I am not shy about being a skeptic; it's how I've fashioned a livelihood. But at some point there is a responsibility for the identifier of problems to give some thought to solutions. My bathroom-floor moment was actually an unwelcome phone-call moment. This was in Las Vegas back in 2009. I was at a conference and, as a paid speaker, felt obliged to join my hosts for a bit of the nightlife. In fact, I was so generous, I did not return to my room until five-thirty a.m., because that's simply the kind of guy I am. At seven a.m., I was awakened by the phone.

It was Ian Wolfman, CMO of MEplusYOU (then imc2). I had never heard of him, but he invited me to come downstairs for the morning keynote. The speaker, he said, had built his business around the very precepts I'd been espousing in my journalism. I, in turn, invited Ian to go fuck himself. Then I hopped into the shower. I was a bit wobbly, but, motivated by God knows what, ventured downstairs for the keynote.

Good move. The speaker was Doug Levy, wearing the most wrinkled suit I had ever seen, offering solid data and business protocols that put flesh on my skeletal ideas. It was a match made in hangover. This book is the result of a collaboration that began that day.

We have something else in common: spouses who support us every which way (including, where necessary, medicinal doses of ridicule). My wife, Milena, has been not so much supporting me as leading me by the hand through my own personal Shift. From critic to consultant. From prophet of doom to prophet of profit. From curmudgeon to . . . well, that's a work in progress. Milena recognized before I did that, by definition, the Cassandra industry is a finite proposition. She (being charitable here) encouraged me to think beyond chaos. In fact, it went like this: As she turned the last page of *The Chaos Scenario*, I asked her if she regarded me as a major genius or simply a genius.

In her charming Eastern European accent, she replied: "Da, Garfield, you are a genius. But you didn't say vat is next."

ACKNOWLEDGMENTS

This book is the product of many years of thinking and doing, but it was also brought to life as a publishing project in a preposterously brief amount of time. This imposed a certain pressure on the situation, and your authors responded by sharing the wealth. We cannot possibly express enough thanks to those who devoted time, energy, ideas and criticism under onerous deadlines. Nor can we adequately rank their contributions, so we will not even attempt to do so. The following alphabetical list is our pale attempt to acknowledge the ample, generous and sometimes heroic support of our friends, colleagues, clients, subjects and loved ones:

Brad Anderson; Lee Applbaum; John Battelle; Brad Berens; Jonah Berger; Pete Blackshaw; Rusty Blazenhoff; Marc Blumberg; Jana Boone; Rex Briggs; Kevin Brown; Rugger Burke; Kathleen Burr; Angie Byrnes; Brooke Carey; Dwayne Chambers; Brian Chin; Scott Chin; Bill Clark; Vanessa Colella; Bill Daddi; Michael Davis; James Dix; Michael Donnelly; Jesse Eisenberg; Hensley Evans; Joel Ewanick; Ken Fadner; Adam Ferrier; Greg Gable; Luis Gaitan; Milena Garfield; Kristen Gastler; Joel Gehman; Jim Geikie; Shane Ginsberg; Seth Godin; Samuel T. Gosling; Marla Gottschalk; Jim Greenwood; Jim Gregory; John Harker; Jeremy Heimans; Kevin Hochman; Tony Hsieh; Ariana Huffington; Michael Jedrzejewski;

Nick Jonas; Karen Keon; Abbey Klaassen; Jeff Klein; Anthony Krinsky; Alyce, Jordan and Taylor Levy; Brian Levy; Joanne and Steve Levy; Bob Liodice; John Mackey; Joe Mandese; Kristi Maynor; Mark McKinney; Evelyn Henry Miller; Modesto Modique; Karen Nelson-Field; Scott Olrich; Dara O'Rourke; K. D. Paine; Geoff Precourt; Alison Provost; Rahul Purini; Doug Rauch; Augie Ray; Fred Reichheld; Joey Reiman; John Replogle; David Rogers; Jeffrey Rohrs; Steve Rosenbaum; Eric Ryan; Rafe Sagalyn; Bria Sandford; Rick Sapio; Alfredo Sarria; Bonnie Sayers; Kyle Schlegel; Mona Seif; Andy Sernovitz; Leslie Shaffer; Ron Shaich; Casey Sheehan; Brian Shin; Simon Sinek; Raj Sisodia; Morgan Spurlock; Rand Stagen; Thales Teixeira; Brett Thomas; Eduardo Tobon; Joe Tripodi; Michele Trowbridge; Karri Valenzuela; Nick Vlahos; Rick Voirin; Ralf VonSosen; Heath Wade; John Wallis; Duncan Watts; Will Weisser; Miry Whitehill; Ken Wilber; Ian Wolfman; and Adrian Zackheim.

NOTES

CHAPTER 1: GOOD-BYE TO ALL THAT
Apocalypse Now

1. "Most Watched TV Finales." *Huffington Post*. N.p., May 15, 2010. http://www.aoltv.com/2010/05/15/most-watched-tv-finales/
2. http://www.seat42f.com/nielsen-tv-ratings-for-04092012.html
3. Seidman, Robert. "DVR Penetration Grows to 39.7% of Households, 42.2% of Viewers." *TV by the Numbers*. N.p., Mar. 23, 2011. http://tvbythenumbers.zap2it.com/2011/03/23/dvr-penetration-grows-to-39-7-of-households-42-2-of-viewers/86819/
4. Anderson, Nate. "DVR Commercial Skipping: 50% or 70%? Depends on Whom You Ask." *Ars Technical*. Dec. 2, 2008. http://arstechnica.com/uncategorized/2008/12/dvr-commercial-skipping-50-or-97-depends-on-whom-you-ask/
5. "Newspaper Circulation Volume." *Newspaper Circulation Volume*. 2012. http://www.naa.org/Trends-and-Numbers/Circulation/Newspaper-Circulation-Volume.aspx
6. Conaghan, Jim. "2011 Newspaper Circulation Numbers." E-mail received August 29, 2012.
7. http://www.strategyanalytics.com/default.aspx?mod=pressreleaseviewer&a0=5268
8. "Digital Music Report 2009." International Federation of the Phonograph Industry. http://www.ifpi.org/content/library/DMR2009.pdf
9. Edmonds, Rick, Guskin, Emily, and Rosenstiel, Tom. *"Newspapers: By the Numbers."* The State of the News Media 2011: An Annual

Report on American Journalism. 2011. http://stateofthemedia.org/
2011/newspapers-essay/data-page-6/

10. http://www.the-numbers.com/market/

11. 2011 J.P. Morgan Media Forecast.

12. "Report: How Americans Are Spending Their Media Time . . . and Money." Nielsenwire. Feb. 9, 2012. http://blog.nielsen.com/ nielsenwire/online_mobile/report-how-americans-are-spending -their-media-time-and-money/

13. Indvik, Lauren. "Ebook Sales Surpass Hardcover for First Time in US." *Mashable Business.* June 17, 2012. http://mashable.com/2012/ 06/17/ebook-hardcover-sales/

You'll Wonder Where Your Money Went

14. "Top 10 Toothpaste Brands." *Advertising Age*, Sept. 24, 2001.

15. Siegel, Bill. "What Happens When You Stop Marketing? The Rise and Fall of Colorado Tourism." Mar. 18, 2009. http://www.denver .org/tourismpays/The-Rise-and-Fall-of-Colorado-Tourism.pdf

16. Garfield, Bob. *And Now a Few Words from Me: Advertising's Leading Critic Lays Down the Law, Once and for All.* (New York: McGraw-Hill, 2003).

17. Edwards, Jim. "P&G to Lay Off 1,600 After Discovering it's Free to Advertise on Facebook." *Business Insider.* Jan. 30, 2012. http:// articles.businessinsider.com/2012-01-30/news/31004736_1 _advertising-digital-media-procter-gamble

Who Is This Person the Supreme Court Says You Are?

18. "Legendary Steve Jobs Quotes." *Exception Magazine.* Oct. 6, 2011. http://exceptionmag.com/moxie/tech-and-toys/0002270/legendary -steve-jobs-quotes

19. Shaw, George Bernard. "Maxims for Revolutionists." 1903.

CHAPTER 2: THE RELATIONSHIP ERA

1. Bruno, Ken. "Panera Bread: Making Dough Despite Tough Times." *Forbes.* Oct. 19, 2010. http://www.forbes.com/sites/marketshare/ 2010/10/19/panera-bread-making-dough-despite-tough-times/

2. http://www.nasdaq.com/symbol/pnra

Dialing for Scholars

3. Sheth, Jagdish and Parvatiyar, Atul. "Relationship Marketing in Consumer Markets: Antecedents and Consequences." *Journal of the Academy of Marketing Sciences.* 1995.

4. Harker, Michael John and Egan, John. "The Past, Present and Future of Relationship Marketing." *Journal of Marketing Management.* 2006.

Butterfly Wings

5. http://ubykotex.com/the_mission

CHAPTER 3: TRUST ME

1. "Tribune Company Makes Investment in Journatic." *Tribune Company.* Apr. 23, 2012. http://www.prnewswire.com/news -releases/tribune-company-makes-investment-in-journatic -148539645.html
2. "Switcheroo." *This American Life.* WBEZ. June 30, 2012.
3. Fourcher, Mike. "Why I Am Resigning from Journatic." *Vouchification.* July 14, 2012. http://blog.fourcher.net/2012/07/14/ why-i-am-resigning-from-journatic/
4. Moos, Julie. "Chicago Tribune Discovers Plagiarism, Suspends Work with Journatic." *Poynter.* July 13, 2012. http://www.poynter. org/latest-news/mediawire/180888/chicago-tribune-stops-using -journatic/

There Is Trust and There Is Trust

5. Grimes, Marisa. "Nielsen: Global Consumers' Trust in 'Earned' Advertising Grows in Importance." *Nielsen.* Apr. 10, 2012. http:// www.nielsen.com/us/en/insights/press-room/2012/nielsen-global -consumers-trust-in-earned-advertising-grows.html
6. Ibid.
7. http://www.perdue.com/Corporate/Our_Story/

City Hall Is Now a Soft Target

8. Mirkinson, Jack. "Rush Limbaugh Advertisers Keep Leaving Show in Wake of Sandra Fluke Comments." *Huff Post Media.* Mar. 6, 2012. http://www.huffingtonpost.com/2012/03/06/rush-limbaugh -advertisers-leave-show-fluke_n_1323358.html
9. "Meat Scandal Sizzles After Claims." *Sina English.* Mar. 17, 2011. http://english.sina.com/china/p/2011/0316/364588.html
10. "Accusations of Intimidation in the Wake of China Train Crash." *Australia Network News.* Aug. 2, 2011. http://www.youtube.com/ watch?v=treob5xouBo

What Time Is It? It's Chart Time!

11. "2010 Edelman Trust Barometer Executive Summary." *Edelman.* 2010. http://www.edelman.com/trust/2010/docs/2010_trust _barometer_executive_summary.pdf

The Three Cs of Trust

12. "The New York Times Completes Research on 'Psychology of Sharing.'" *New York Times*. July 13, 2011. http://phx.corporate-ir.net/phoenix.zhtml?c=105317&p=irol-newsArticle&ID=1584873

Brand Power

13. "Methodology Overview." *CoreBrand*. 2012. http://www.corebrand.com/brandpower/methodology-overview
14. Mulligan, Thomas S. and Kraul, Chris. "Texaco Settles Race Bias Suit for $176 Million." *Los Angeles Times*. Nov. 16, 1996. http://articles.latimes. com/1996-11-16/news/mn-65290_1_texaco-settles-race-bias-suit

CHAPTER 4: ON PURPOSE

1. Carroll, Dave. "United Breaks Guitars." July 2009. http://www.davecarrollmusic.com/music/ubg/song1/
2. http://en.wikipedia.org/wiki/United_Breaks_Guitars
3. "Alternatives to Lawsuits." *Social Strategy*. http://www.socialstrategy1.com/wp-content/uploads/2010/03/case_studies/cs-alternatives_to_lawsuits.pdf

Happiness in a Carton

4. Steinert-Threlkeld, Tom. "Happy Birthday, Zappos: A Billion-Dollar Business Built on . . . Culture?" *ZD Net*. June 1, 2009. http://www.zdnet.com/blog/btl/happy-birthday-zappos-a-billion-dollar-business-built-on-culture/18960
5. Austin, Scott and Geron, Tomio. "Zappos Not Exactly Another Dot-Com Triumph for Sequoia." *Venture Capital Dispatch*. July 22, 2009. http://blogs.wsj.com/venturecapital/2009/07/22/zappos-not-exactly-another-dot-com-triumph-for-sequoia/
6. McFarland, Keith. "Why Zappos Offers New Hires $2,000 to Quit." *Bloomberg Businessweek*. Sept. 16, 2008. http://www.businessweek.com/stories/2008-09-16/why-zappos-offers-new-hires-2-000-to-quitbusinessweek-business-news-stock-market-and-financial-advice
7. Wauters, Robin. "Amazon Closes Zappos Deal, Ends Up Paying $1.2 Billion." AOL. Nov. 2, 2009. http://techcrunch.com/2009/11/02/amazon-closes-zappos-deal-ends-up-paying-1-2-billion/

If You Don't Believe Us, Ask Chuck

8. *Forbes*, Sept. 17, 2001.
9. "Schwab Acquires U.S. Trust." *CNN Money*. Jan. 13, 2000. http://money.cnn.com/2000/01/13/deals/schwab/
10. S., Michelle. "Reviving Customer Relationships and Growth by Focusing on Loyalty." Satmetrix Net Promoter Community. Jan. 27,

2009. http://www.netpromoter.com/netpromoter_community/blogs/conference_sf_2009/tags/schwab

11. Li, Charlene. "Charles Schwab on Building Customer Relationships with Net Promoter." *Altimeter.* Jan. 26, 2009. http://www.altimetergroup.com/2009/01/charles-schwab-on-building-customer-relationships-with-net-promoter.html

12. "Schwab Earns Highest Customer Loyalty Ranking Among Brokerage and Investment Firms in Satmetrix Net Promoter's 2010 Industry Report." *Business Wire.* Mar. 25, 2010. http://www.businesswire.com/news/home/20100325005295/en/Schwab-Earns-Highest-Customer-Loyalty-Ranking-Brokerage

Putting Your Money Where Your Mouth Is

13. http://www.patagonia.com/us/patagonia.go?assetid=2047
14. http://www.patagonia.com/us/patagonia.go?assetid=1960
15. "Keeping Employees Happy: Sportswear Firm Beefs Up Benefits to Boost Worker Contentment." *Los Angeles Times.* Apr. 23, 1989. http://articles.latimes.com/1989-04-23/news/mn-1760_1_patagonia-capilene-day-care-center
16. http://www.patagonia.com/us/patagonia.go?assetid=67517
17. Chouinard, Yvon and Brown, Michael S. "Going Organic: Converting Patagonia's Cotton Product Line." *Journal of Industrial Ecology.* Feb. 8, 2008. http://onlinelibrary.wiley.com/doi/10.1162/jiec.1997.1.1.117/abstract
18. Garfield, Bob and Levy, Doug. "The Dawn of the Relationship Era." *Advertising Age.* Jan. 2, 2012. http://adage.coverleaf.com/advertisingage/20120102?pg=11#pg11
19. Nudd, Tim. "Ad of the Day: Patagonia: The Brand Declares War on Consumerism Gone Berserk, and Admits Its Own Environmental Failings." *Adweek.* Nov. 28, 2011. http://www.adweek.com/news/advertising-branding/ad-day-patagonia-136745
20. Jaffe, Joseph. *Join the Conversation: How to Engage Marketing-Weary Consumers with the Power of the Community.* (New York: Wiley, 2007), p. 226.

I Deep Fry, Therefore I Am

21. http://www.krispykreme.com/about-us/mission-and-vision

Love Is Blue (Cheese)

22. http://chickenanywhere.com/our-mission.php

While You're Out, Grab Me a Skinny Latte Grande and a Reputation

23. http://www.altria.com/en/cms/About_Altria/Our_Mission_and_Values/default.aspx
24. http://www.agsm.edu.au/bobm/teaching/BE/Cases_pdf/enron-code.pdf

25. Dorfman, Lori; Cheyne, Andrew; Friedman, Lissy C.; Wadud, Asiya; and Gottlieb, Mark. "Soda and Tobacco Industry Corporate Social Responsibility Campaigns: How Do They Compare?" *PLOS Medicine.* June 19, 2012. http://www.plosmedicine.org/article/info% 3Adoi%2F10.1371%2Fjournal.pmed.1001241

Ad Agencies Against Purpose

26. Kwong, Jessica. "Keeping Your Home Clean and 'Green'." Forbes. com. Mar. 8, 2010. http://www.forbes.com/2010/03/08/method -clorox-green-technology-ecotech-cleaning.html
27. Address to the Association of National Advertisers, Nov. 8, 2010.

Lumbering Along

28. http://www.ncaa.org/wps/wcm/connect/public/ncaa/pdfs/2012/ decertification+marucci+cat-5+and+black+bats

CHAPTER 5: SUSTAIN

1. "The Customer Experience Index, 2011." Forrester Research. Jan. 11, 2011.
2. Patel, Kunur. "AT&T's Strategy to Win Consumer Love: Be Human." AdAge Digital. Apr. 18, 2012. http://adage.com/article/ special-report-digital-conference/strategy-win-consumer-love -human/234204/
3. Ibid.
4. Ibid.

Plant Turbines

5. "General Electric Company." Knowmore.org. May 8, 2010. http:// knowmore.org/wiki/index.php?title=General_Electric_Company
6. Kocieniewski, David. "GE's Strategies Let it Avoid Taxes Altogether." *New York Times.* Mar. 24, 2011. http://www.nytimes .com/2011/03/25/business/economy/25tax.html?pagewanted=all

CHAPTER 6: THE SECRET SECRET

1. "The Biggest Brand Manager in the Land Speaks on Purpose-Driven Marketing." *AdExchanger.* Oct. 19, 2010. http://www .adexchanger.com/advertiser/purpose-driven-marketing/
2. Ibid.

Bomb the Ban

3. Spurlock, Morgan. *The Greatest Movie Ever Sold.* 2011.
4. Mickle, Tripp. "Procter & Gamble Formally Announce Details of USOC Partnership." Sports Business Daily.com. Sept. 1, 2009. http://www.sportsbusinessdaily.com/Daily/Issues/2009/09/Issue

-240/Olympics/Procter-Gamble-Formally-Announce-Details-Of
-USOC-Partnership.aspx.

5. "P&G Becomes Global Olympic Sponsor." *Associated Press*. July 28,
    2010. http://sports.espn.go.com/oly/news/story?id=5416272

Damn You, Google Search!

6. Thomas, Katie. "After Long Fight for Inclusion, Women's Ski Jumping
    Gains Olympic Status." *New York Times*. Apr. 6, 2011. http://www.
    nytimes.com/2011/04/07/sports/skiing/07skijumping.html?adxnnl=1&
    adxnnlx=1345579271-mQRDkK/wxQi+1KkabdMUfQ

But Wait . . .

7. S., Tara. "Boca." Yelp. Jan. 11, 2012. http://www.yelp.com/biz/boca
    -cincinnati?sort_by=date_desc

Waterproof

8. "Diana Nyad Back in U.S. After Abandoning Cuba to Florida
    Swim." CNN Health. Aug. 9, 2011. http://www.cnn.com/2011/
    HEALTH/08/09/nyad.103.mile.swim/index.html

9. "Diana Nyad Quits Cuba-to-Florida Swim." CBSSports.com.
    Sept. 25, 2011. http://www.cbsnews.com/2100-400_162-
    20111366.html

10. Sedensky, Matt. "Diana Nyad's Swim from Cuba Ends After Threats
    from Sharks and Storms." *Huffington Post*. Aug. 21, 2012. http://
    www.huffingtonpost.com/2012/08/21/diana-nyads-swim-cuba_n
    _1817669.html

The Bully Pulpit

11. http://industry.shortyawards.com/category/social_media_in_real
    _life/yQ/secret-mean-stinks

12. Edwards, Jim. "Facebook Claims It Increased P&G's Deodorant
    Sales by 9%." *Business Insider*. Feb. 1, 2012. http://articles.
    businessinsider.com/2012-02-01/news/31011971_1_facebook-page
    -ipo-filing-social-network

13. Spears, Lee. "Facebook Value Tops $100B Based on Private Market."
    Bloomberg. Feb. 9, 2012. http://www.bloomberg.com/news/
    2012-02-09/facebook-value-tops-100b-based-on-private-market.html

CHAPTER 7: THAT THING CALLED LIKE

1. "The Meaning of Like." ExactTarget. 2011. http://www.exacttarget
    .com/resources/SFF10_highres.pdf

2. Klaassen, Abbey. "How Two Coke Fans Brought the Brand to
    Facebook Fame." AdAge Digital. Mar. 16, 2009. http://adage.com/
    article/digital/coke-fans-brought-brand-facebook-fame/135238/

The Virtual Country That Refreshes

3. The blunder ended up as a bonanza for both Coke and Pepsi. It triggered a wave of line extensions that pushed other competitors off the supermarket shelves.

My Name's Everyman; I Carry a Badge

4. Lury, Celia. *Consumer Culture*. (Wiley, 2010).
5. Dittmar, Helga and Pepper, Lucy. "Materialistic Values, Relative Wealth, and Person Perception: Social Psychological Belief Systems of Adolescents from Different Socio-Economic Backgrounds." In Floyd Rudmin and Marsha Richins (eds.), *Meaning, Measure, and Morality of Materialism*. (Provo, UT: Association for Consumer Research and School of Business, Queen's University, 1992), pp. 40–45.
6. Schau, Hope Jensen and Gilly, Mary C. "We Are What We Post? Self-Presentation in Personal Web Space." *Journal of Consumer Research*. Vol. 30, No. 3. 2003. http://marketing.eller.arizona.edu/docs/papers/Hope%20Schau/Schau_Gilly_JCR_2003.pdf

Your Basic Win-Win-Win-Win

7. Kessler, Andy. "The Button That Made Facebook Billions." *Wall Street Journal*. Feb. 2, 2012. http://online.wsj.com/article/SB1000142405297020465290457719699220306957.html
8. Ibid.

On the Other Hand . . .

9. Interview with Jeffery Rohrs,
10. Creamer, Matthew. "Study: Only 1% of Facebook 'Fans' Engage with Brands." AdAge Digital. Jan. 27, 2012. http://adage.com/article/digital/study-1-facebook-fans-engage-brands/232351/

Trailing Indicator?

11. Franzen, Jonathan. "Liking Is for Cowards. Go for What Hurts." *New York Times*. May 28, 2011. http://www.nytimes.com/2011/05/29/opinion/29franzen.html?pagewanted=all

CHAPTER 8: THE SHIFT
How to Venn Friends and Influence People
Step 1: Listen.

1. http://meero.worldvision.org/faq_categorie.php?categorieID=6#92
2. http://www.worldvision.org/content.nsf/about/who-we-are

Step 2: Define social personality.

3. Lawrence, D. H., letter, Dec. 12, 1915, to author Katherine
   Mansfield. In George J. Zytaruk and James T. Boulton (eds.),
   The Letters of D. H. Lawrence, Vol. 2. (Cambridge University
   Press, 1981).

Step 4: Lead the conversation.

4. Nudd, Tim. "Chrysler Throws Down an F-bomb on Twitter."
   Adweek. Mar. 9, 2011. http://www.adweek.com/adfreak/chrysler
   -throws-down-f-bomb-twitter-126967

Step 5: Ignite and invite action.

5. "Wimpy South Africa Reaches Out to Visually Impaired with
   'Braille Burger'." Globalpost. Jan. 16, 2012. http://www.globalpost
   .com/dispatches/globalpost-blogs/weird-wide-web/wimpy-braille
   -burger-south-africa-sesame-seeds-blind
6. http://www.youtube.com/watch?v=5YAchE0-o-o
7. http://en.wikipedia.org/wiki/Ben_Franklin_effect

Step 6: Inspire greater collaboration.

8. http://politics.nytimes.com/election-guide/2008/results/states/
   CA.html

CHAPTER 9: DO'S AND DON'TS AND . . . NO, REALLY, DON'TS
Kick Me

1. "#McDStories, McDonald's Twitter Hashtag Promotion, Goes
   Horribly Wrong." *Huffington Post*. Jan. 23, 2012. http://www
   .huffingtonpost.com/2012/01/23/mcdstories-twitter-hashtag_n
   _1223678.html#s630540&title=CATE_STORM
2. Ibid.
3. Hill, Kashmir. "#McDStories: When a Hashtag Becomes a
   Bashtag." *Forbes*. Jan. 24, 2012. http://www.forbes.com/sites/
   kashmirhill/2012/01/24/mcdstories-when-a-hashtag
   -becomes-a-bashtag/
4. https://twitter.com/BigHFish/status/161796168391720960
5. https://twitter.com/alexroth3/status/161873590881497088
6. https://twitter.com/Undateable_Girl/status/159745858789851136
7. https://twitter.com/Muzzafuzza/status/159740460842225664
8. https://twitter.com/deepstereo/status/161196285112754176
9. "#McDStories: When A Hashtag Becomes A Bashtag." *Los Angeles
   Times*, Jan. 24, 2012.

10. McNaughton, Marissa. "Lessons from the #McDStories Promoted Trend Controversy." *Realtime Report.* Jan. 24, 2012. http:// therealtimereport.com/2012/01/24/lessons-from-the-mcdstories -promoted-trend-controversy/

Tilting at Epidemics

11. "The Psychology of Sharing: Why Do People Share Online", CIG The New York Times Customer Insight Group. July 13, 2011. http:// nytmarketing.whsites.net/mediakit/pos/.
12. Watts, Duncan J. Peretti, Jonah and Frumin Michael. "Viral Marketing for the Real World." University of Copenhagen, July 29, 2010. http://www.itu.dk/people/rkva/2010-Summer-IM/readings/ watts2007_viralmarketing.pdf.

Johnny Appleseed

13. Watts, Duncan J. Peretti, Jonah and Frumin Michael. "Viral Marketing for the Real World." University of Copenhagen, July 29, 2010. http://www.itu.dk/people/rkva/2010-Summer-IM/readings/ watts2007_viralmarketing.pdf.

Now, Here Are Those Do's We Promised You

14. Quinton, Brian. "Betty Crocker Hits Sweet Spot with How-to Cake Videos." Chief Marketer Network. Jan. 3, 2012. http://chiefmarketer .com/video/betty-crocker-hits-sweet-spot-how-cake-videos

Curate

15. "MTV Veteran and User-Generated Video Expert, Steve Rosenbaum, to Present at the AlwaysOn Stanford Summit." Magnify.net. 2012. http://finance.paidcontent.org/paidcontent/news/ read?GUID=2758142
16. Garfield, Bob. "Project Baby Slobs Shows That Sharing Works Better Than Branding." AdAge Blogs. Feb. 24, 2012. http://adage .com/article/bob-garfield/twins-eating-lunch-shows-sharing-works/ 232920/

Genuine Naugahyde

17. http://www.youtube.com/watch?v=Ldq2tNLRDwA
18. http://www.youtube.com/watch?annotation_id=annotation _847643&feature=iv&src_vid=Ldq2tNLRDwA&v=pAUawDGycCU
19. Lundin, Steve. "RIM Botches PR Stunt Announcing New Marketing Campaign." May 7, 2012. http://www.stevelundin.com/
20. Blazenhoff, Rusty. "Southwest Flight Attendants Make Galley Food Recipes with Passengers." *Laughing Squid.* Mar. 14, 2012. http:// laughingsquid.com/southwest-flight-attendants-make-galley-food -recipes-with-passengers/

CHAPTER 10: BANK AND TRUST

1. Nuckols, Ben. "Molly Katchpole, Recent College Grad and Part Time Nanny, Helps End Bank of America Fee." *Huffington Post.* Nov. 3, 2011. http://www.huffingtonpost.com/2011/11/03/molly -katchpole-recent-co_n_1074481.html
2. "Our Opinion: Make Big Banks Pay Price for Their Greed." *State Journal-Register.* Oct. 12, 2011. http://www.sj-r.com/breaking/ x153927903/Our-Opinion-Make-big-banks-pay-price-for-their-greed
3. Miller, Sunlen. "Durbin to Bank of America Customers: 'Get the Heck Out of That Bank'." *ABC News.* Oct. 3, 2011. http://abcnews .go.com/blogs/politics/2011/10/durbin-to-bank-of-america- customers-get-the-heck-out-of-that-bank/
4. Jones, Susan. "Obama: Banks Don't Have 'Inherent Right' to 'Certain Amount of Profit'." Cnsnews.com. Oct. 4, 2011. http:// cnsnews.com/news/article/obama-banks-dont-have-inherent-right -certain-amount-profit
5. Kim, Susanna. "Bank of America Cancels $5 Fee." *ABC News.* Nov. 1, 2011. http://abcnews.go.com/Business/bank-america-drops-plan -debit-card-fee/story?id=14857970

CHAPTER 11: THIS COULD BE THE END OF A PREVIOUSLY VERY GOOD RELATIONSHIP

This Could Be the End of a Previously Very Good Relationship

1. http://ww5.komen.org/AboutUs/OurWork.html
2. http://ww5.komen.org/uploadedFiles/Content/AboutUs/Financial/ 2011%20Komen%20Financial%20Statements%20FINAL(3).pdf
3. http://en.wikipedia.org/wiki/Nancy_Brinker
4. Belluck, Pam. "Cancer Group Halts Financing to Planned Parenthood." *New York Times.* Jan. 31, 2012. http://www.nytimes .com/2012/02/01/us/cancer-group-halts-financing-to-planned -parenthood.html
5. Powers, Lindsay. "Fewer Sign up to Race for the Cure." *USA Today.* Apr. 16, 2012. http://www.usatoday.com/NEWS/usaedition/ 2012-04-16-Race-for—Cure_ST_U.htm
6. "Johnson & Johnson Ranks as Most Reputable U.S. Company in Reputation Institute's 2010 Reputation Pulse Study; AIG Ranks Last." *PR Newswire.* Apr. 20, 2010. http://www.prnewswire.com/ news-releases/johnson—johnson-ranks-as-most- reputable-us-company-in-reputation-institutes-2010-reputation -pulse-study-aig-ranks-last-91589399.html
7. http://reputationinstitute.com/frames/events/2012_US_RepTrak _Press_Release_April_3.pdf

Just Sew It

8. Greenhouse, Steven. "Nike Shoe Plant in Vietnam Is Called Unsafe for Workers." *New York Post.* Nov. 8, 1997. http://www.nytimes.com/1997/11/08/business/nike-shoe-plant-in-vietnam-is-called-unsafe-for-workers.html?pagewanted=all&src=pm

Paging Isaac Newton

9. http://www.apple.com/pr/library/2012/01/24Apple-Reports-First-Quarter-Results.html
10. "Transcript: President Obama Delivers State of the Union Speech." *CNN Politics.* Jan. 24, 2012. http://articles.cnn.com/2012-01-24/politics/politics_sotu-transcript_1_applause-fair-share-hard-work/7?_s=PM:POLITICS
11. "Truth Squad: Steve Jobs' Jobs vs. Obama's Jobs." *CNN Politics.* Jan. 25, 2012. http://articles.cnn.com/2012-01-25/politics/politics_truth-squad-steve-jobs_1_steve-jobs-stimulus-bill-stimulus-money?_s=PM:POLITICS
12. Yee, Lee Chyen. "Rights Group Says Apple Suppliers in China Breaking Labor Laws." Reuters. Jun. 28, 2012. http://in.reuters.com/article/2012/06/28/us-apple-china-suppliers-idINBRE85R0EA20120628

INDEX